Guided Korean Writing for the Real World

실생활 한국어 쓰기 길잡이 (초-중급)

Angela Lee-Smith (Yale University)

Kijoo Ko (University of California, Berkeley)

Angela Lee-Smith (Yale University)

Angela Lee-Smith, Ph.D., is a Senior Lector II of Korean in the Department of East Asian Languages and Literatures at Yale University. Her pedagogical practice and research interests include multiliteracies, interculturality, project-based learning, curriculum design, assessments, and teacher education.

Kijoo Ko (University of California, Berkeley)

Kijoo Ko, Ph.D., is a lecturer of Korean in the Department of East Asian Languages and Cultures at the University of California, Berkeley. Her research focuses on bilingual language organization, second language acquisition, teaching Korean as a foreign language, and computer-aided language learning.

Guided
Korean Writing
for the Real World

실생활 한국어 쓰기 길잡이 (초-중급)

1판 1쇄 발행 2024년 1월 15일

지은이 Angela Lee-Smith, Kijoo Ko

펴낸이 박영호
기획팀 송인성, 김선명, 김선호
편집팀 박우진, 김영주, 김정아, 최미라, 전혜련, 박미나
관리팀 임선희, 정철호, 김성언, 권주련

펴낸곳 (주)도서출판 하우
주소 서울시 중랑구 망우로68길 48
전화 (02)922-7090
팩스 (02)922-7092
홈페이지 http://www.hawoo.co.kr
e-mail hawoo@hawoo.co.kr
등록번호 제2016-000017호

값 39,000원
ISBN 979-11-6748-118-4 13710

Guided Korean Writing for the Real World

실생활 한국어 쓰기 길잡이 (초-중급)

Introduction

In today's digital age, written communication has become an integral part of our lives, spanning various platforms such as email, chat, text messaging, and social media. To navigate these real-life writing situations effectively, this book offers step-by-step writing activities designed to equip Korean language learners at elementary to intermediate-low proficiency levels with essential written communication skills.

The book focuses on five critical functions of writing: Introduction and Explanation, Inquiry and Request, Narration and Description, Evaluation and Report, and Argument and Persuasion. Each function is explored through five comprehensive lessons, providing learners with a well-rounded understanding of Korean writing.

Structure of the Book:

1. **Learning Objectives and Can-Do Statements:**
   Every lesson begins with clearly defined learning objectives and corresponding can-do statements. These objectives outline the goals you will achieve by the end of each lesson, while the can-do statements set performance standards for your writing skills.

2. **Useful Vocabulary, Grammar, and Expressions:**
   This section presents a comprehensive list of expressions and grammar patterns commonly used in the writing topics covered in each lesson. By familiarizing yourself with these essential language elements beforehand, you will better comprehend the writing samples and prepare for subsequent writing activities.

3. **Writing Samples:**
   Each lesson features two or three writing samples that serve as both examples to learn from and benchmarks for assessing your writing skills. After completing a lesson, you can aim to write at a similar level to these samples, using them as a guide to track your progress and identify areas for improvement.

4. Pre-writing Exercises:

The pre-writing exercises form the initial guided steps towards achieving the intended learning goals. During this stage, you will brainstorm ideas, organize your thoughts, practice relevant vocabulary and expressions, and draft sentences or paragraphs.

5. Interpersonal Writing:

Real-life written communication often involves exchanging ideas, messaging, and corresponding with others. This section is dedicated to exercises that simulate interpersonal communication scenarios. By practicing written exchanges likely to occur in daily life, you will enhance your interpersonal communicative skills in writing.

6. Presentational Writing:

Frequently, you will need to write and present information to an audience of readers, such as creating website content, writing advertisements or reports, or developing PowerPoint materials. This section offers writing tasks that replicate real-life situations and are tailored for an audience of readers.

7. Writing Tips:

In this section, you will find explanations of writing conventions, mechanics, idiomatic expressions, phrases, and cultural practices. These tips provide valuable insights into effective writing and help you develop a deeper understanding of the Korean language.

With its practical approach and comprehensive structure, "Korean Writing for the Real World" is an invaluable resource for Korean language learners seeking to enhance your written communication skills. Whether you are a beginner or an intermediate learner, this book will guide you through step-by-step activities that simulate real-life writing tasks, preparing you to confidently navigate written communication in various contexts.

Functions and Topics

Function/ Genre	Lesson	Topic
Introduction and Explanation	1.1	자기 소개 Self-Introduction
	1.2	취미와 관심 Hobbies and Interests
	1.3	하루 일과 Daily Routines
	1.4	집과 학교 Home and School
	1.5	길 안내 Giving Directions
Inquiry and Request	2.1	초대 Invitations
	2.2	예약과 약속 Making reservations and Appointments
	2.3	동아리 가입 Joining Clubs
	2.4	이메일과 편지 Emails and Letters
	2.5	물건 사기 Buying Things
Narration and Description	3.1	일기 Personal Daily Journal
	3.2	축하와 감사 Congratulations and Thanks
	3.3	거절과 사과 Refusals and Apologies
	3.4	양식 작성 Filling Out Forms
	3.5	계획 Plans
Evaluation and Report	4.1	장소 후기 Reviewing Places
	4.2	쇼핑 후기 Shopping Reviews
	4.3	활동 후기 Reviewing Activities
	4.4	감상 후기 Appreciation Reports
	4.5	여행 후기 Reviewing Trips
Argument and Persuasion	5.1	찬성과 반대 For and Against
	5.2	조언 Advice
	5.3	주장과 제안 Argument and Suggestion
	5.4	설득 Persuasion
	5.5	안내문 Notices

Contents

1.1. 자기 소개 Self-Introduction

Lesson Objectives

- Writing a self-introduction
- Writing to present and exchange information about oneself

Can-Do

- I can introduce myself using vocabulary and expressions related to who I am and what I do.
- I can exchange basic information about myself (name, nationality, occupation, hometown, hobby, family, etc.) using a mixture of practiced or memorized words, phrases, and simple sentences.
- I can present basic information about myself in simple sentences.

 Useful Vocabulary, Grammar, and Expressions

1. Vocabulary

(1) ☐ 이름 given name/first name ☐ 성 last name/family name ☐ 성명 full name (last name + first name)

☐ 국적 nationality ☐ 고향 hometown ☐ 가족 family

☐ 엄마/어머니 mom/mother ☐ 아빠/아버지 dad/father ☐ 부모님 parents

(2)	언니 older sister for female	누나 older sister for male	오빠 older brother for female

(2)
언니 older sister for female   누나 older sister for male   오빠 older brother for female
형 older brother for male   여동생 younger sister   남동생 younger brother
동생 younger sibling   할머니 grandmother   할아버지 grandfather

(3)
전공 major   부전공 minor   직업 occupation
취미 hobby   특기 specialty   동호회 hobby/leisure club
꿈 career dreams   계획 plans   동아리 school/extracurricular club

2. Grammar

① 제 이름은 N(name)예요/이에요/입니다. My name is N(name).

② 저는 N(name)(이)라고 해요/합니다. I am called N(name).

③ N(country) 사람이에요/입니다. I am a(n) N(country) person.

④ N(country/city)에서 왔어요/왔습니다. I came from N(country/city).

⑤ N(country/city/housing)에 살아요/삽니다. I live in N(country/city/housing).

⑥ 부모님은 N(country/city)에 계세요/계십니다. My parents are in N(country/city).

⑦ 저는 형(or 오빠)/누나 (or 언니) number 명하고 남/여동생 number 명이 있어요/있습니다.
I have # older brothers/sisters and # younger brothers/sisters.

⑧ 저는 N(occupation)예요/이에요/입니다. I am a(n) N(occupation).

⑨ N(work/school)에 다녀요/다닙니다. I attend N(work/school).

⑩ N(subject)을/를 공부해요/공부합니다. I study N(subject).

⑪ N(subject)을/를 전공해요/전공합니다. I am majoring in N(subject).

⑫ 전공은 N(subject)예요/이에요/입니다. My major is N(subject).

⑬ 저는 N(hobby/specialty)을/를 좋아해요/좋아합니다. I like N(hobby/specialty).

⑭ N(hobby/specialty)을/를 해요/합니다. I do/play N(hobby/specialty).

⑮ N(occupation)을/를 할 거예요/겁니다. I will do N(occupation).

⑯ N(occupation)이/가 되고 싶어요/싶습니다. I want to become a(n) N(occupation).

⑰ -고 싶다/싶어 하다 to want to

⑱ -(으)려고 하다, -(으)ㄹ 계획이다 to plan to

⑲ -(으)면 좋겠다 to hope/wish to

3. Expressions

① 안녕하세요/안녕하십니까? Hello?

② 처음 뵙겠습니다. Nice to meet you. (Lit. It is my first time meeting you.)

③ (만나서) 반가워요/반갑습니다. Glad (to meet you).

④ 이름이 뭐예요? What is your name?

⑤ 성함이 어떻게 되세요? What is your name? *(honorific)*

⑥ 취미가 뭐예요? What is your hobby?

⑦ 무슨 동아리 (활동) 해요? What club are you in?

⑧ 전공이 뭐예요? What is your major?

⑨ 무슨 일 하세요? What do you do for a living?

⑩ 어디에 살아요/사세요? Where do you live?

⑪ 가족이/형제가 어떻게 되세요? How many family members/siblings do you have?

Writing Samples

1. Rebecca is a senior at a college in the U.S. and is going to Korea for one year to learn the Korean language and culture as a postgraduate fellow.

(1) She will live with a host family and now writes a brief self-introduction via the online application platform to the host mother.

안녕하세요?

저는 레베카 스미스예요. 미국 사람이에요. 지금 미국 보스턴 대학교 4학년이에요. 동양학을 전공해요. 그리고 국제학을 부전공해요.

제 고향은 미시간이에요. 미시간에 부모님과 동생이 있어요.

저는 이번 여름에 한국 명성 대학교에서 공부할 거예요. 이번 여름에 호스트 가족하고 지내게 돼서 아주 기뻐요. 제 취미는 요리예요. 한국 음식을 정말 좋아해요. 이번 여름에 호스트 가족하고 한국 음식을 같이 만들고 싶어요.

보스턴 Boston, 동양학 Asian Studies, 국제학 International Studies, 부모님 parents,

호스트 가족 host family, −게 돼서 기쁘다 to be glad to

(2) This time, Rebecca writes an email to a professor of political science at the Myungsung University, where she will study abroad for a year after this summer. In this email, Rebecca briefly introduces herself and her academic plans.

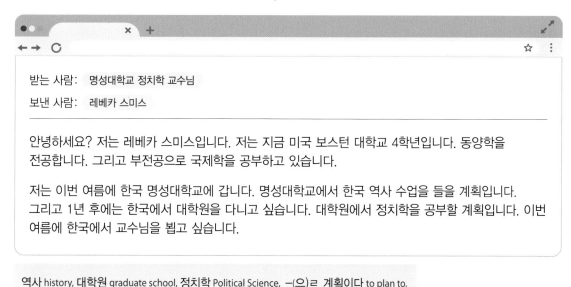

받는 사람: 명성대학교 정치학 교수님

보낸 사람: 레베카 스미스

안녕하세요? 저는 레베카 스미스입니다. 저는 지금 미국 보스턴 대학교 4학년입니다. 동양학을 전공합니다. 그리고 부전공으로 국제학을 공부하고 있습니다.

저는 이번 여름에 한국 명성대학교에 갑니다. 명성대학교에서 한국 역사 수업을 들을 계획입니다. 그리고 1년 후에는 한국에서 대학원을 다니고 싶습니다. 대학원에서 정치학을 공부할 계획입니다. 이번 여름에 한국에서 교수님을 뵙고 싶습니다.

역사 history, 대학원 graduate school, 정치학 Political Science, −(으)ㄹ 계획이다 to plan to,

뵙다 to see someone (honorific), −고 싶다 to want to

2. Your local Korean community has a social media site, *Humans of K-Community*, that introduces its members. They just posted an introduction of each new member of the community. Meet the new member Dira. Here is her self-introduction post.

Humans of K-Community

새 회원을 소개합니다!

안녕하세요? 처음 뵙겠습니다.

제 이름은 디라 사바위입니다. 한국대학교 경제학과 1학년 학생입니다.

저는 사우디아라비아 사람입니다. 어렸을 때 우리 가족은 아버지의 일 때문에 한국에서 2년 동안 살았습니다.

저는 한국 친구들과 한국 문화, 한국 음악, 한국 음식 모두 아주 좋아합니다. 그래서 한국에 다시 오고 싶었습니다. 지금은 서울에서 살고 있습니다. 정말 행복합니다.

여러분하고 우리 문화 센터에서 자주 만나면 좋겠습니다.

반갑습니다. 잘 부탁드립니다.

새 new, 회원 member, 경제학 Economics, 문화 culture, -고 있다 to be -ing, 때문에 because of, 사우디아라비아 Saudi Arabia

Pre-Writing Exercises

1. You are signing up for an online pen pals club in a joint program with Hankuk University in Korea, one of the exchange programs of your college.

List information about yourself for the pen pal matching process.

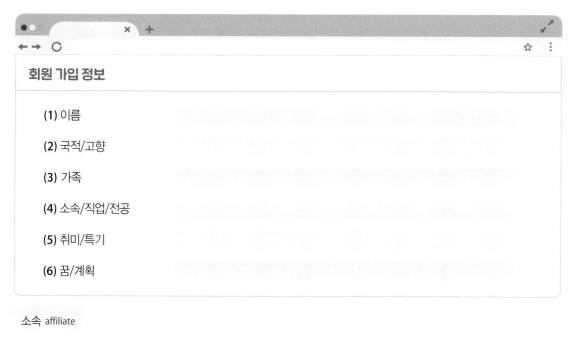

회원 가입 정보

(1) 이름

(2) 국적/고향

(3) 가족

(4) 소속/직업/전공

(5) 취미/특기

(6) 꿈/계획

소속 affiliate

2. You are taking a summer class at the Korean Culture and Language Study Institute at Hankuk University in Korea. You made a lot of new friends in your class.

(1) Introduce a couple of them to your pen pal, Eunjoo Oh.

리사 존슨
전공: 역사, 부전공: 한국학
대학교: 미시간 대학교 3학년
고향: 시카고

트로이 잭슨
전공: 정치학, 부전공: 동아시아학
대학교: 하와이 대학교 4학년
고향: 뉴욕

You

You

(2)

영화 감상	음악	수영
요리	독서	?

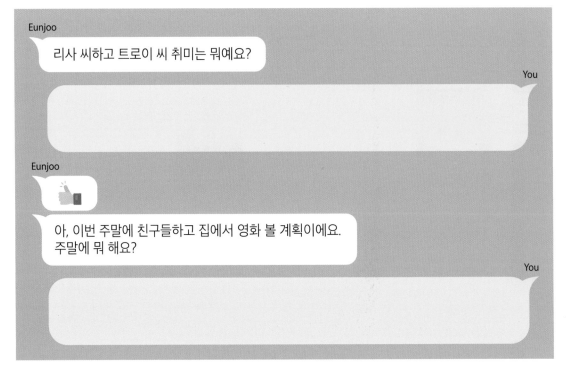

Eunjoo

리사 씨하고 트로이 씨 취미는 뭐예요?

You

Eunjoo

아, 이번 주말에 친구들하고 집에서 영화 볼 계획이에요.
주말에 뭐 해요?

You

Interpersonal Writing

1. You are a newcomer to an online community, HanK-Cafe, where Hankuk University students can join and share their interests, questions, and opinions in general. It is your first time joining this chat platform. Enjoy your first communication with the members.

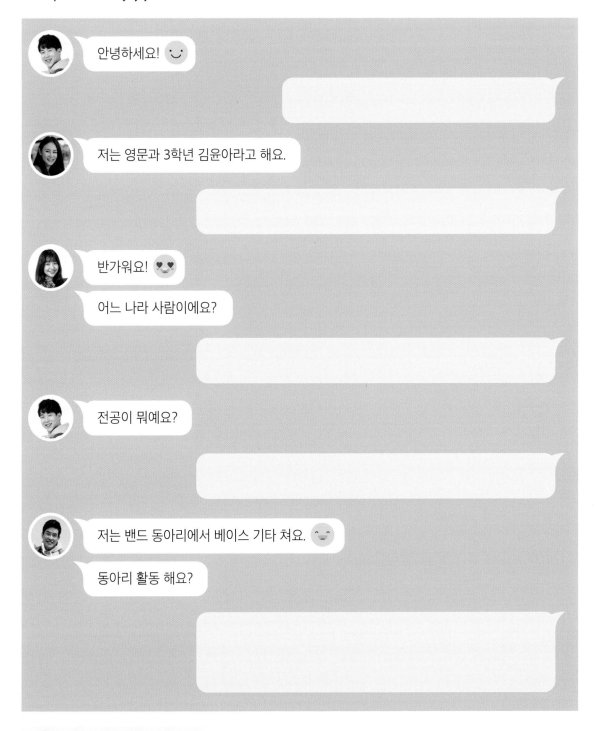

영문과 Department of English Literature

2. A staff member of the Korean Cultural Center (한국문화원) sent you an email. Read the email and reply appropriately.

보내기

보내는사람	
받는 사람	
제목	

안녕하세요?

저는 한국 문화 센터에서 일하는 김수진입니다. 우리 문화 센터에 오신 것을 환영합니다.

새 회원님들을 우리 센터 홈페이지에 소개하고 싶습니다. 회원님의 자기 소개를 이메일로 보내 주세요. 사진도 한 장 보내 주세요.

감사합니다.

김수진 드림

(Write your reply)

Presentational Writing

1. This summer, you are going to Korea as an exchange student and staying with a host family. Write a text message introducing yourself to the host family. Include the following information:

   ◦ Your name and what you do
   ◦ More about yourself (e.g., your hobbies, things you enjoy doing, family, etc.)
   ◦ Your plans (things you want to do, plan to do, etc.)

2. You are going to Korea this summer to study abroad. Write a brief email introducing yourself to the professor you will be meeting. Include the following information:

   ◦ Your name, what you do
   ◦ More about yourself (e.g., your areas of interest)
   ◦ Your plans

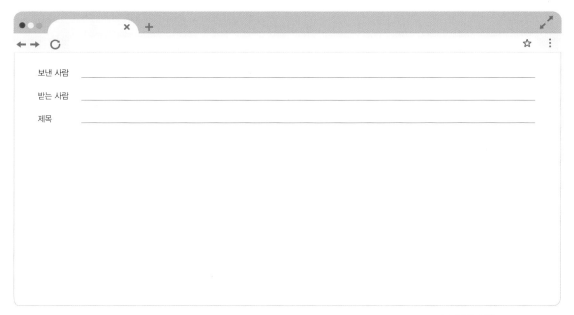

이름 쓰기

Writing Names

A person's name in Korea is written 성+이름 (last name + first name) with no spacing between last and first name).

ex 이정재, 전지현, 현빈

However, if it is necessary to distinguish between last and first names clearly, it can be written separately with a space.

ex 남궁현 (last name 남, first name 궁현) vs 남궁 현 (last name 남궁, first name 현)

선우빈 (last name 선, first name 우빈) vs 선우 빈 (last name 선우, first name 빈)

For foreign names, there are no rules or guidelines. However, it is common practice to write first name + space + last name.

ex 제인 스미스, 수잔 김

 ## -아/어요 vs -(스)ㅂ니다

Informal vs Formal Polite Styles

Though both styles are polite, the difference is the degree of formality. In public or formal writing, the formal polite style -(스)ㅂ니다 is used, and in private, personal, or casual daily interactions, the informal polite style -아/어요 is commonly used. That being said, occasionally, these two styles may be mixed in writings to small degrees, especially in semi-(in)formal interpersonal writings.

문장 부호: 마침표 (.) vs 물음표 (?) vs 느낌표 (!)
Punctuation Marks: Period vs Question mark vs Exclamation mark

In writing, 안녕하세요 is used as a greeting phrase, which means "Hi, Greetings, Hello, or How are you?" in English. So, . (마침표 period), ? (물음표 question mark) or even ! (느낌표 exclamation mark) can be used.

ex 안녕하세요./안녕하세요?/안녕하세요!

In general, when the level of question is weak (in other words, when you're not really asking because you don't know), a period can be used instead of a question mark.

However, -(스)ㅂ니까?, as in 안녕하십니까?, is a formal style ending for a question. Therefore, in this case, a question mark is always used.

ex 안녕하십니까?

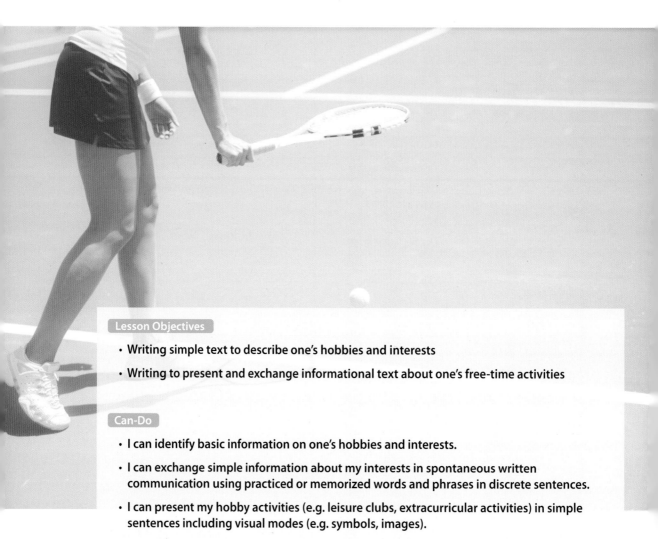

1.2. 취미와 관심 Hobbies and Interests

Lesson Objectives

- Writing simple text to describe one's hobbies and interests
- Writing to present and exchange informational text about one's free-time activities

Can-Do

- I can identify basic information on one's hobbies and interests.
- I can exchange simple information about my interests in spontaneous written communication using practiced or memorized words and phrases in discrete sentences.
- I can present my hobby activities (e.g. leisure clubs, extracurricular activities) in simple sentences including visual modes (e.g. symbols, images).

 ## Useful Vocabulary, Grammar, and Expressions

1. Vocabulary

(1) Sports

☐ 수영 swimming	☐ 테니스 tennis	☐ 요가 yoga
☐ 태권도 Taekwondo	☐ 조깅 jogging	☐ 스키 ski
☐ 스노보드 snowboard	☐ 자전거 bicycle	☐ 골프 golf

| 볼링 bowling | 축구 soccer | 배구 volleyball |
| 농구 basketball | 야구 baseball | 탁구 table tennis |

(2) Instruments

피아노 piano	바이올린 violin	첼로 cello
기타 guitar	드럼 drum	클라리넷 clarinet
색소폰 saxophone	플루트 flute	

(3) Hobbies

요리 cooking	쇼핑 shopping	여행 travel
낚시 fishing	영화 movie	음악 music
독서 reading	그림 drawing/painting	춤 dancing
노래 singing	게임 gaming	

(4) "To play" verbs

- N(을/를)+ 하다 to do

수영 swimming	조깅 jogging	축구 soccer
야구 baseball	농구 basketball	태권도 Taekwondo
요가 yoga	게임 game	노래 song

- N(을/를)+ 치다 to hit

테니스 tennis	탁구 table tennis	배드민턴 badminton
골프 golf	볼링 bowling	피아노 piano
기타 guitar	드럼 drum	

- N(을/를)+ 타다 to ride

| 스키 ski | 스케이트 skate | 스노보드 snowboard |
| 자전거 bicycle | | |

- N(을/를)+ 켜다 to play (string instrument)

| 바이올린 violin | 첼로 cello | 하프 harp |

- N(을/를)+ 불다 to blow (wind instrument)

| 클라리넷 clarinet | 트럼펫 trumpet | 색소폰 saxophone |
| 플루트 flute | | |

(5) Frequencies

- ☐ 매일 everyday
- ☐ 주말 weekend
- ☐ 자주 often

- ☐ 매주 every week
- ☐ 가끔 sometimes
- ☐ 주로 mostly

- ☐ 매월/매달 every month
- ☐ 보통 usually
- ☐ N에 Korean number + 번 time(s) per

2. Grammar

① -기 -ing, -는 것 doing

② -(으)러 가다/오다 to go/come in order to

③ -기도 하고 -기도 하다 to do either or/and

④ -아/어 보고 싶다 to want to try

3. Expressions

① 취미가 어떻게 되세요? What is your hobby? (more polite than "취미가 뭐예요?")

② 관심이 있어요/많아요. I have interest in / I have a lot of interest in.

Writing Samples

1. David is taking Korean 1B (Elementary Korean II) this semester.

(1) David uploaded his first posting to introduce himself on the "Get to Know" section of the Korean 1B course website.

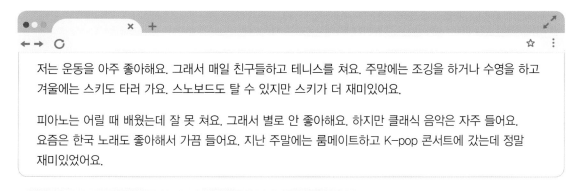

저는 운동을 아주 좋아해요. 그래서 매일 친구들하고 테니스를 쳐요. 주말에는 조깅을 하거나 수영을 하고 겨울에는 스키도 타러 가요. 스노보드도 탈 수 있지만 스키가 더 재미있어요.

피아노는 어릴 때 배웠는데 잘 못 쳐요. 그래서 별로 안 좋아해요. 하지만 클래식 음악은 자주 들어요. 요즘은 한국 노래도 좋아해서 가끔 들어요. 지난 주말에는 룸메이트하고 K-pop 콘서트에 갔는데 정말 재미있었어요.

―거나 either, 어릴 때 when I was young, 별로 not particularly, 요즘 recently

(2) David also read a couple of posings that his classmates uploaded.

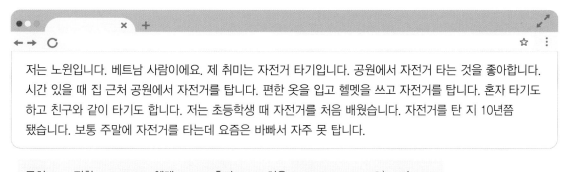

저는 노원입니다. 베트남 사람이에요. 제 취미는 자전거 타기입니다. 공원에서 자전거 타는 것을 좋아합니다. 시간 있을 때 집 근처 공원에서 자전거를 탑니다. 편한 옷을 입고 헬멧을 쓰고 자전거를 탑니다. 혼자 타기도 하고 친구와 같이 타기도 합니다. 저는 초등학생 때 자전거를 처음 배웠습니다. 자전거를 탄 지 10년쯤 됐습니다. 보통 주말에 자전거를 타는데 요즘은 바빠서 자주 못 탑니다.

근처 near, 편한 comfortable, 헬멧 helmet, 혼자 alone, 처음 for the first time, ―(으)ㄴ 지 since

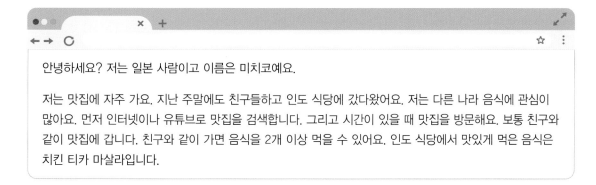

안녕하세요? 저는 일본 사람이고 이름은 미치코예요.

저는 맛집에 자주 가요. 지난 주말에도 친구들하고 인도 식당에 갔다왔어요. 저는 다른 나라 음식에 관심이 많아요. 먼저 인터넷이나 유튜브로 맛집을 검색합니다. 그리고 시간이 있을 때 맛집을 방문해요. 보통 친구와 같이 맛집에 갑니다. 친구와 같이 가면 음식을 2개 이상 먹을 수 있어요. 인도 식당에서 맛있게 먹은 음식은 치킨 티카 마살라입니다.

맛집 gourmet restaurant, 먼저 first of all, 검색하다 to search (on the internet), 이상 more than ―(으)ㄹ 수 있다 can, 방문하다 to visit, 인도 식당 Indian restaurant, 치킨 티카 마살라 chicken tikka masala

2. Jane is a freshman in college who is interested in joining clubs on campus. While walking on campus, she saw this poster about a club on the bulletin board.

한국 아카펠라 동아리
한가락

K-POP을 좋아합니까?
함께 K-POP을 부르고 싶습니까?
그럼 '한가락' 동아리에 오세요.
노래를 잘 못해도 괜찮습니다.
오디션도 없습니다.

3월 10일 오후 5시에 학생회관 1층
305호로 오세요.

동아리 extracurricular club, —아/어도 even though

3. The Korean Cultural Center at Maisha's local community is hosting its annual enrollment period for hobby clubs. Read the following information.

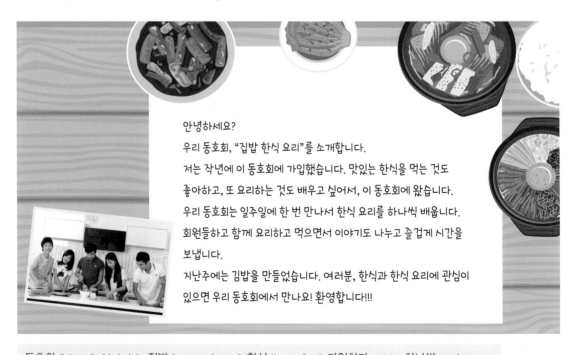

안녕하세요?
우리 동호회, "집밥 한식 요리"를 소개합니다.
저는 작년에 이 동호회에 가입했습니다. 맛있는 한식을 먹는 것도 좋아하고, 또 요리하는 것도 배우고 싶어서, 이 동호회에 왔습니다.
우리 동호회는 일주일에 한 번 만나서 한식 요리를 하나씩 배웁니다.
회원들하고 함께 요리하고 먹으면서 이야기도 나누고 즐겁게 시간을 보냅니다.
지난주에는 김밥을 만들었습니다. 여러분, 한식과 한식 요리에 관심이 있으면 우리 동호회에서 만나요! 환영합니다!!!

동호회 (leisure/hobby) club, 집밥 homemade meal, 한식 Korean food, 가입하다 to join, 하나씩 one by one, 회원 member, 나누다 to share, 환영하다 to welcome

Pre-Writing Exercises

1. You and your classmate are doing a name-hobby matching activity in the Korean 1B class. Based on the picture, fill out the pair activity chart about each one's hobby.

춤 추기   사진 찍기   베이킹   영화 보기   음악 듣기   그림 그리기

브리아나

메이

마크

샌드라

호세

김 선생님

ex 브리아나의 취미는 <u>베이킹</u> 이에요. 브리아나는 <u>빵 만드는 것</u> 을 좋아해요.

❶ 메이의 취미는 _____. 메이는 _____.

❷ 마크의 취미는 _____. 마크는 _____.

❸ 샌드라의 취미는 _____. 샌드라는 _____.

❹ 호세의 취미는 _____. 호세는 _____.

❺ 김 선생님의 취미는 _____. 김 선생님은 _____.

2. You want to join a dance club at college and are told that there is a K-dance club. After sending an email to Diana, who is a leader of the K-dance club, you receive a response from her.

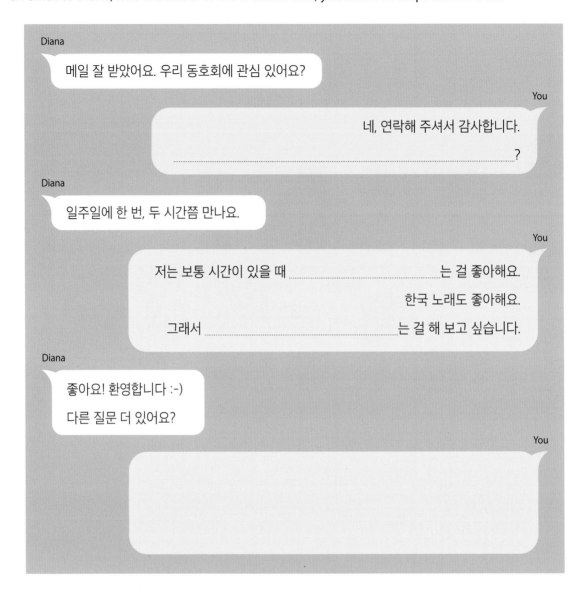

Diana

메일 잘 받았어요. 우리 동호회에 관심 있어요?

You

네, 연락해 주셔서 감사합니다.

_____?

Diana

일주일에 한 번, 두 시간쯤 만나요.

You

저는 보통 시간이 있을 때 _____는 걸 좋아해요.

한국 노래도 좋아해요.

그래서 _____는 걸 해 보고 싶습니다.

Diana

좋아요! 환영합니다 :-)
다른 질문 더 있어요?

You

3. Your high school encourages each student to join a hobby club. Refer to a sample below and fill out a survey paragraph form about your interest so that the teacher can assign you to a matching club.

> 제 취미는 영화 감상입니다. 코미디 영화하고 액션 영화를 좋아합니다. 무서운 영화는 별로 좋아하지 않습니다. 주로 미국 영화나 유럽 영화를 보지만, 유명한 한국 영화도 보고 싶습니다. 친구들하고 재미있는 영화도 보고, 영화에 대한 세미나도 하면 좋겠습니다.

영화 감상 watching movie, 유명하다 to be famous, −에 대한 about, −(으)면 if

Write a paragraph about what you are interested in.

Interpersonal Writing

1. You are planning to go to Korea next summer and live with a host family. Today, you are matched with the Kim family and you write a letter to them introducing yourself, your family, and your interests.

김 선생님 가족분들께,

올림

2. You and your new roommates are making a weekend plan together. Respond to the text messages in the group chat room.

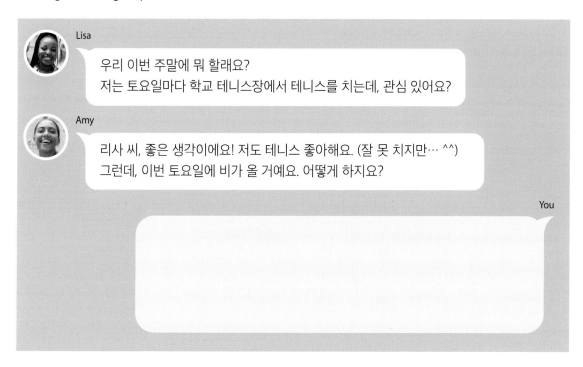

Lisa

> 우리 이번 주말에 뭐 할래요?
> 저는 토요일마다 학교 테니스장에서 테니스를 치는데, 관심 있어요?

Amy

> 리사 씨, 좋은 생각이에요! 저도 테니스 좋아해요. (잘 못 치지만… ^^)
> 그런데, 이번 토요일에 비가 올 거예요. 어떻게 하지요?

You

3. You are writing an inquiry email to the coordinator of a hobby club you would like to join at work. Introduce yourself and write about your interests. Make sure to include several questions about the club.

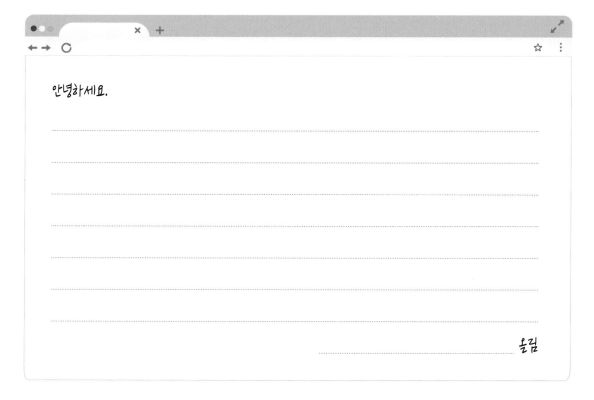

안녕하세요.

올림

Presentational Writing

1. You went to the local cultural center to join a hobby club this summer. Fill out a membership application form and find out which clubs are available to join.

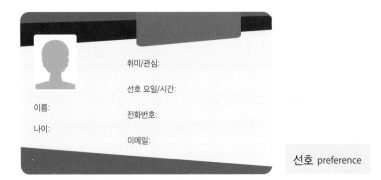

2. Post a photo with a brief description about your hobby on a hobby forum of a social network site "Hobby World."

3. Your hobby club is promoting new members. Produce a poster or brochure that contains general information about your club.

Writing Tips

외래어와 외국어 표기

Notation of Loanwords and Foreign words

보스턴? vs 보스톤?, 배드민턴? vs 배드민톤?

Loadwords and foreign words are written according to pronunciation, not spelling. In the English-speaking world, there are many place names that end in -ton, but they are also written in '-턴' according to the same principle. For example, American cities such as Washington, Boston, and Houston are written as 워싱턴, 보스턴, 휴스턴 in Korean. Badminton, as in "Playing badminton," is the same way- notate as 배드민턴.

There are detailed rules recommended by the National Institute of Korean Language (국립국어원). However, you may refer to this site for a loanword-Korean converter for your reference: http://loanword.cs.pusan.ac.kr/

문자/이메일에 쓰이는 부호와 줄임말

Emoticons and Abbreviations used in Texting/Email

Below are the emoticons and abbreviations that are commonly used for informal text messages. Be careful when using these to someone who is older or higher than you as it may sound too casual. You should not use these for formal messages.

Guess what each emoticon/abbreviation means.

:-)	^^	^^;;	>_<		
ㅋㅋ	ㅎㅎ	ㅍㅎㅎ	ㄷㄷ	ㅜㅜ	ㅠㅠ
ㅇㅋ	ㅇㅇ	ㅎㅇ	ㅂㅂ	ㄱㅅ	ㅈㅅ
ㅇㄷ					

1.3. | 하루 일과 Daily Routines

Lesson Objectives

- Writing simple text to describe one's daily routine
- Writing to present and exchange informational text about one's daily life, daily routines, diary, and notes in authentic settings

Can-Do

- I can ask and express basic information on daily activities and schedules (e.g. routines, dates, times, places, activities, events, to-do lists, etc.).
- I can present a simple narrative of what I do daily in short messages and notes using vocabulary, phrases, and expressions I learned.
- I can present basic information about myself in simple sentences.
- I can post highlights of my daily activities using short messages, emojis, and memes on texting/social media in simple sentences.

 ## Useful Vocabulary, Grammar, and Expressions

1. Vocabulary

(1) Time

☐ 오전 AM	☐ 오후 PM	☐ 시 hour
☐ 분 minute	☐ 시간 hours	☐ 동안 for, during
☐ 밤 night	☐ 아침 morning	☐ 점심 lunch time

☐ 저녁 evening

(2) Days and dates

☐ 월요일 Monday   ☐ 화요일 Tuesday   ☐ 수요일 Wednesday

☐ 목요일 Thursday   ☐ 금요일 Friday   ☐ 토요일 Saturday

☐ 일요일 Sunday   ☐ 주말 weekend   ☐ 주중/평일 weekday

(3) Daily routines

☐ 일어나다 to get up/wake up   ☐ 샤워하다 to take shower   ☐ 세수하다 to wash face

☐ 이(를) 닦다 to brush teeth   ☐ 옷(을) 입다 to put clothes on   ☐ 청소하다 to clean

☐ 빨래하다 to do laundry   ☐ 요리하다 to cook   ☐ 일하다 to work

☐ 아침/점심/저녁 식사하다 to have breakfast/lunch/dinner   ☐ 출근/퇴근하다 to go/leave work

☐ 돌아오다 to return/come back home   ☐ 자다 to sleep   ☐ 쉬다 to rest

☐ 장(을) 보다 to go grocery shopping   ☐ 연습하다 to practice   ☐ 항상 always

☐ 늦게 late   ☐ 일찍 early   ☐ 보통 usually

☐ 자주 often

2. Grammar

① -고 나서 doing and then, -(으)ㄴ 다음에/ 후에 after doing, N 후에 after N

② -기 전에 before doing, N 전에 before N

③ -자마자 as soon as doing

④ N마다 every N

⑤ 얼마나 자주 how often

3. Expressions

① 보통 주말에 뭐 해요? What do you usually do on weekends?

② 어떻게 시간을 보내요? How do you spend your time?

③ 하루 일과가/스케줄이 어떻게 돼요? What's your daily routine/schedule?

Writing Samples

1. The following is Jenny's To-Do list for this Saturday, her birthday. Jenny has invited friends to her home for a sleepover.

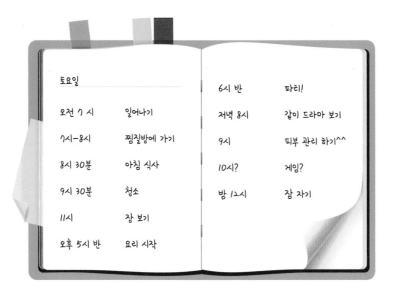

토요일	
오전 7시	일어나기
7시-8시	찜질방에 가기
8시 30분	아침 식사
9시 30분	청소
11시	장 보기
오후 5시 반	요리 시작

6시 반	파티!
저녁 8시	같이 드라마 보기
9시	피부 관리 하기^^
10시?	게임?
밤 12시	잠 자기

할 일 to-do, 피부 관리 skin care, 찜질방 JJimjilbang (Korean-style spa)

2. Jenny had a great time with her friends, who came over for a sleepover on her birthday. She wrote a brief daily journal and posted to her social media site.

오늘은 제 생일이에요! 친구들하고 같이 맛있는 생일 케이크도 먹고, 드라마도 봤어요. 드라마 보고 나서 피부관리도 했어요. ^^

3. Sunny is a K-Pop idol. Her manager recently shared her daily routines for her world fans.

시간	일과
5:00	일어나기
5:30–6:30	요가하기
6:30–7:00	아침 식사
7:00–9:00	댄스 스튜디오에서 춤 연습하기
9:00–11:00	녹음 스튜디오에서 노래 연습하기
11:00–2:00	TV쇼 인터뷰
3:00–6:00	콘서트 준비하기
7:00–8:00	저녁 식사하고 좀 쉬기
8:00–9:00	라디오 팟캐스트 하기
9:00–11:00	뮤직 비디오 찍기

Pre-Writing Exercises

1. List your daily routines and To-Do list in your daily planner.

TO DO LIST

요일	할 일
오전 _____ 시 _____ 분	일어나기 (일어나요)
	아침 식사 (아침 식사해요)
저녁 8시	
	잠 자기

2. Write a daily journal about what you did today.

_____ 년 _____ 월 _____ 일 _____ 요일

아침 9시에 일어났어요. 일어나고 나서 _____

_____

_____

_____

_____

_____

_____

_____

_____

_____

Interpersonal Writing

1. Your language exchange partner (penpal) asked you the following questions. Reply to your penpal by responding to the questions.

❶ 보통 평일에는 뭐 해요?

❷ 주말에는 어떻게 시간을 보내요?

2. The roommate matching process for your dormitory has started. Fill in the form about your daily routine and schedule for best matching.

❶ 보통 몇 시에 일어납니까?

❷ 보통 몇 시에 잡니까?

❸ 보통 어디에서 공부합니까?

❹ 동아리 활동은 주로 어디에서 언제 합니까?

❺ 음악을 들을 때 헤드폰이나 이어폰을 씁니까?

❻ 샤워나 목욕은 보통 언제 합니까?

❼ 보통 친구들과 집에서 만납니까?

❽ 보통 주말에는 어떻게 시간을 보냅니까?

❾ 청소는 얼마나 자주 합니까?

3. Your friends posted memes that describe how they feel at the end of a Friday. Post your meme with a simple captioning.

> 드디어 금요일이에요. 너무 피곤해요. 아, 정말 쉬고 싶어요.

Presentational Writing

1. You are a week-long summer camp counselor for children in grades 4-6 in local communities. This camp is a residential camp at the local school site. Make a daily schedule for one entire day. Post that schedule and activities to share with your campers and parents.

.... 요일

시간	활동
	일어나기
	잠 자기

Writing Tips

날짜와 시간 쓰기
Writing Dates & Time

In Korean convention, the date format starts with the year, followed by the month, day, and then the day of the week. In contrast, English date format typically begins with the day of the week, followed by the month, day, and year.

> **ex** 2025년 10월 30일 토요일 (Korean)
> 2025. 10. 30. 토 (Korean)
> Saturday, October 30, 2025 (English)

When you write time in Korean, there are several ways as in examples.

> **ex** 오후 5시 30분 (Korean)
> 오후 5:30 (Korean)
> 5:30 PM (English)

> **ex** 평일에는 보통 오전 8시에 아침 식사해요.
> 평일에는 보통 8:00 오전에 아침 식사해요. (X)

목록에 쓰이는 –기 vs –(으)ㅁ
Nominalization for List of Activities

When writing a list of activities, -기 is used for routines/activities in present or future, whereas -(으)ㅁ is commonly used for past activities (things already done).

> **ex** 저녁 먹기 (저녁 먹어요)
> 저녁 먹음 (저녁 먹었어요)
>
> 친구들 만나기 (친구들 만나요)
> 친구들 만남 (친구들 만났어요)
>
> 영화 보기 (영화 봐요)
> 영화 봄 (영화 봤어요)

It is also very common to write just the noun part in -기, if the verb itself contains a noun.

> **ex** 연습 (연습하기)

1.4. 집과 학교 Home and School

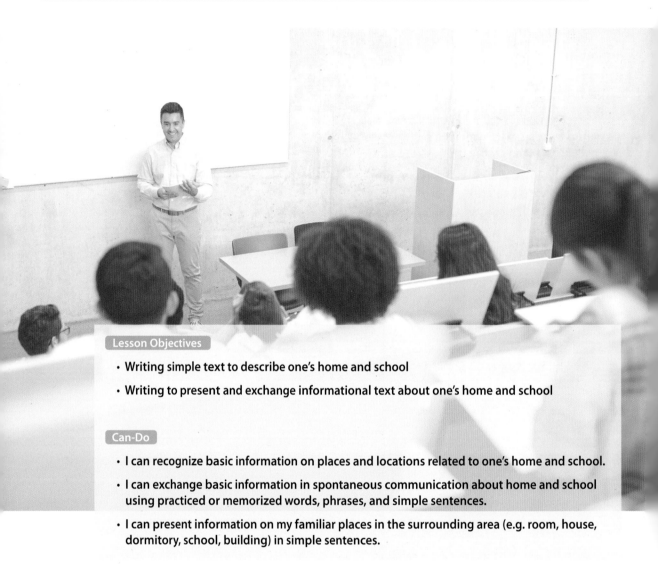

Lesson Objectives

- Writing simple text to describe one's home and school
- Writing to present and exchange informational text about one's home and school

Can-Do

- I can recognize basic information on places and locations related to one's home and school.
- I can exchange basic information in spontaneous communication about home and school using practiced or memorized words, phrases, and simple sentences.
- I can present information on my familiar places in the surrounding area (e.g. room, house, dormitory, school, building) in simple sentences.

⊙ Useful Vocabulary, Grammar, and Expressions

1. Vocabulary

(1) Places

☐ 집 house	☐ 아파트 APT	☐ 방 room
☐ 부엌 kitchen	☐ 거실 living room	☐ 화장실 restroom
☐ 1/2/3층 1st/2nd/3rd floor	☐ 건물 building	☐ 대학교 university

고등학교 high school	중학교 middle school	초등학교 elementary school
캠퍼스 campus	교실 classroom	사무실 office
학생회관 student center	기숙사 dormitory	도서관 library
체육관 gym	책방/서점 bookstore	식당/음식점 restaurant
커피숍/카페 coffee shop	운동장 field	수영장 swimming pool
테니스장 tennis court	볼링장 bowling alley	스케이트장 skating rink
영화관/극장 theater	노래방 karaoke	백화점 department store
시장/마켓 market	편의점 convenience store	가게 store
빵집/제과점 bakery	꽃집 flower shop	우체국 post office
미용실 hair salon	이발소 barber shop	공원 park
역 station	정류장 bus stop	주차장 parking lot

(2) Things

책 book	공책 notebook	책상 desk
탁자 table	의자 chair	가방 bag
필통 pencil case	펜 pen	볼펜 ball pen
연필 pencil	지우개 eraser	침대 bed
책장 bookshelf	옷장 closet	서랍 drawer
시계 watch/clock	그림 drawing	액자 frame
벽 wall	문 door	창문 window
전화(기) telephone	컴퓨터 computer	모니터 monitor
텔레비전 television	소파 sofa	(전)등/램프 lamp
선풍기 fan	에어컨 AC	히터 heater
쓰레기통/휴지통 trash can	칠판 blackboard	

(3) Location

앞 front	뒤 back	옆 side
위 up	아래/밑 under	안/속 inside
밖 outside	왼쪽 left side	오른쪽 right side
가운데 middle	사이 between	건너(편) across
근처 nearby	여기 here	저기 over there
거기 there		

(4) Description

- [ ] 있다 to exist
- [ ] 없다 to not exist
- [ ] 많다 to be many
- [ ] 적다 to be few
- [ ] 크다 to be big
- [ ] 작다 to be small
- [ ] 넓다 to be wide
- [ ] 좁다 to be narrow
- [ ] 높다 to be high
- [ ] 낮다 to be low
- [ ] 예쁘다 to be pretty
- [ ] 아름답다 to be beautiful
- [ ] 가깝다 to be close
- [ ] 멀다 to be far
- [ ] 싸다 to be cheap
- [ ] 비싸다 to be expensive
- [ ] 맛있다 to be delicious
- [ ] 맛없다 to be not delicious
- [ ] 좋다 to be good
- [ ] 나쁘다 to be bad
- [ ] 좋아하다 to like
- [ ] 싫어하다 to dislike
- [ ] 재미있다 to be interesting
- [ ] 재미없다 to be uninteresting
- [ ] 깨끗하다 to be clean
- [ ] 더럽다 to be dirty
- [ ] 조용하다 to be quiet
- [ ] 시끄럽다 to be noisy
- [ ] 편하다 to be convenient
- [ ] 불편하다 to be inconvenient

2. Grammar

① -고 and

② -아/어서 because

③ -지만 however

④ -(으)ㄴ/는데 but *(giving background information)*

3. Expressions

① 어디(에) 있어요? Where is it?

② 뭐(가) 있어요? What is there?

③ 어때요? How is it?

④ 얼마나 걸려요? How long does it take?

⑤ 얼마예요? How much is it?

Writing Samples

1. Junko is an exchange student at Seoul University and just moved to a dormitory. She is describing her room in an email to her mom in Japan who is really curious about the place.

받는 사람: 엄마

엄마,

여기는 제 방이에요. 조금 좁지만 싸고 학교에서 가까워서
좋아요.

방 가운데 책상이 있어요. 책하고 컴퓨터, 전화는 책상 위에
있어요. 창문 앞에는 옷장이 있고, 그 옆에는 침대가 있어요.
옷장하고 침대 사이에 작은 서랍도 있는데, 그 위에 파란 색
전등도 있어요. 그리고, 벽에는 제가 좋아하는 그림들이 있어요.

어때요? 깨끗하고 예쁘지요?

그림 drawing, 파란색 blue color

2. Mark is a junior at Hankook University who is an active member of the University Publicity Club. He recently wrote an article about his campus life in the club newsletter.

저는 한국대학교에 다닙니다. 캠퍼스는 아주 크고 학생들이
많습니다. 기숙사는 조금 비싸지만 깨끗하고 조용합니다.
기숙사 안에 식당이 있는데 음식은 별로 맛이 없습니다.
그래서 주말에는 친구들하고 같이 학교 앞에 있는 식당에
갑니다. 보통 한국 식당과 중국 식당에 가는데, 음식도
맛있고 값도 쌉니다. 그리고 가끔 친구의 아파트에서 음식을
만듭니다.

학교 근처에는 여러 가게들도 많고 버스 정류장과 지하철
역도 가까워서 아주 편합니다. 시장은 좀 멀지만 편의점이
여러 군데 있어서 괜찮습니다. 가끔 쇼핑을 하러 백화점에
가고, 영화 보러 극장에도 갑니다. 차로 10분쯤 걸립니다.
대학 캠퍼스 생활이 정말 재미있습니다.

별로 not really, 여러 several, 군데 place, 정말 really, 생활 life

3. Elin is a junior at Millennium University and needs to move to an apartment near campus next semester. She found an advertisement in a local newspaper looking for tenants.

DAILY NEWS

밀레니엄 대학교 근처 집 렌트

위치: 밀레니엄 대학교 근처
(걸어서 20분, 버스로 5분)

시설: 방 2개, 화장실 1개, 차고 1개

특징: 리모델 된 깨끗한 방, 조용한 동네,
가까운 버스 정류장 / 지하철 역

물/쓰레기 포함, 전기/인터넷 제외

월세: 100만 원

연락처: (935) 382-6704

위치 location, 근처 near, 시설 facility, 차고 garage, 특징 characteristics, 쓰레기 trash, 포함 included, 제외 excluded, 전기 electricity, 연락처 contact

Pre-Writing Exercises

1. You are an RA (residence assistant) at Daehan University. In order to help incoming students, you need to write about your room at Dos Hall in detail and post on the school housing website.

❶ Let's start by listing items in the room.

Q: 방 안에 뭐가 있어요?

A: _____

❷ Now, let's describe where each item above is located in the room. Use location words (e.g., 앞, 뒤, 옆, 위, 밑, 아래) so that your room can be visualized. Finish the paragraph with sentences describing the room in general.

방 안에 _____ 이/가 있어요.

_____ 앞/뒤에 _____ 이/가 있어요.

_____ 에 _____ 이/가 있어요.

_____ 에 _____ 이/가 있어요.

_____ 은/는 _____ 에 있어요.

기숙사 방은 _____. 그리고 _____.

2. Your friend plans to transfer to your college next year and wants to know about the school campus. Write an email describing your campus area.

받는 사람: _____

학교 캠퍼스는 _____.

앞/뒤에 _____.

옆에 _____.

은/는 _____.

학교 근처에 _____.

_____.

_____.

Interpersonal Writing

1. Your classmate Eugene is interested in subletting your APT during the summer. Reply to the text inquiry with appropriate information.

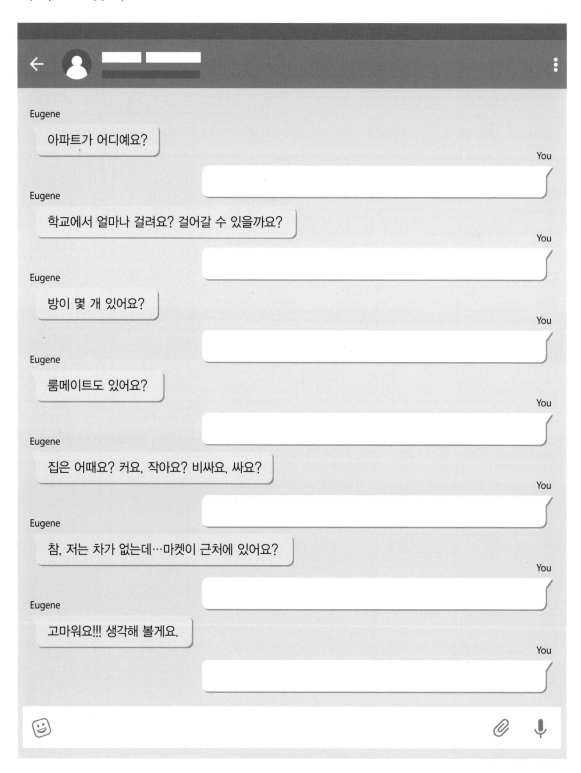

Eugene
> 아파트가 어디예요?

You

Eugene
> 학교에서 얼마나 걸려요? 걸어갈 수 있을까요?

You

Eugene
> 방이 몇 개 있어요?

You

Eugene
> 룸메이트도 있어요?

You

Eugene
> 집은 어때요? 커요, 작아요? 비싸요, 싸요?

You

Eugene
> 참, 저는 차가 없는데…마켓이 근처에 있어요?

You

Eugene
> 고마워요!!! 생각해 볼게요.

You

2. You just moved to college as a freshman. Today, you got an email from your favorite high school teacher. Respond to her by describing your dormitory/campus.

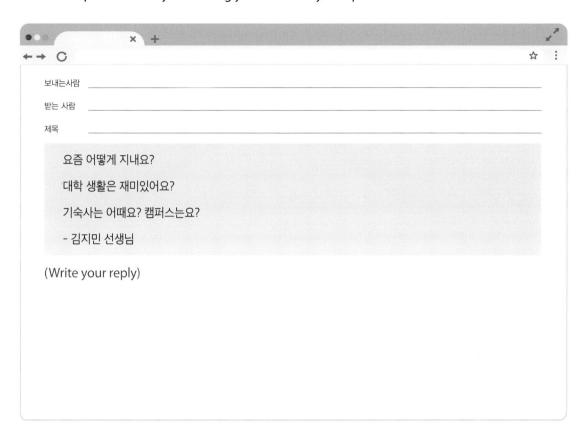

보내는사람 _____

받는 사람 _____

제목 _____

요즘 어떻게 지내요?

대학 생활은 재미있어요?

기숙사는 어때요? 캠퍼스는요?

- 김지민 선생님

(Write your reply)

3. You are writing a birthday card to your friend in another state/country. Ask him/her to visit your school during this coming vacation. Describe the school campus to convince your friend to come and see.

_____ 에게

생일 축하해요! 보고 싶어요!!!

_____

_____

_____

_____

_____ 이/가

1. You are looking for two roommates to share a 3-bedroom APT for the fall semester. Describe the apartment and neighborhood to post a flyer on the campus bulletin board.

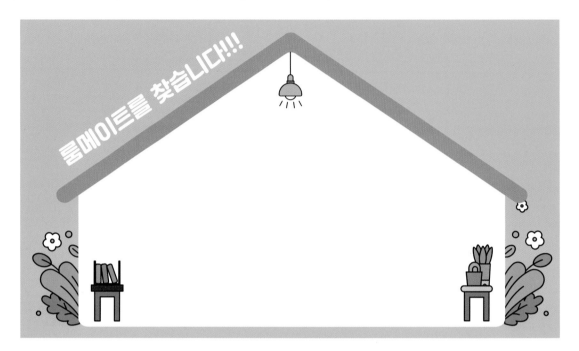

2. You are a member of the school ambassador club "My Daehan" at Daehan University. For the upcoming College Open House Week, you need to create advertising materials about the school.

❶ First, create a flier introducing Daehan University.

❷ As a student attending Daehan University, write an article promoting the school and sharing your college experience. This will be published in the university newspaper.

Writing Tips

 전단지/공고문에 쓰이는 -(으)ㅁ

Nominalization for Flyer/Announcement

For flyers/leaflets, you can use various ending styles such as nouns, verb->noun forms -(으)ㅁ, informal polite style -아/어요, formal polite style -(스)ㅂ니다.

ex 방 렌트
방 렌트함
방 렌트해요
방 렌트합니다

-(으)ㅁ forms are considered to be neutral and can be useful when you need to use verbs or adjectives. When a verb stem ends in a vowel, attach ㅁ to the stem. When a verb stem ends in a consonant, use 음 to it.

ex 구하다 → 구함
있다 → 있음

Recently, young people often use this -(으)ㅁ style on the internet and you need to be careful as it may not sound polite.

룸메이트 구함
Looking for a Roomate

8월부터 12월까지 함께 살
룸메이트를 찾습니다!

월 55만 원 (물/전기 포함)
인터넷은 추가 요금 있음
차로 5분 거리 (Route 63 & 309)
침대, 책상, 의자, 세탁기, 부엌용품 있음

추가 additional, 요금 charge

1.5. | 길 안내 Giving Directions

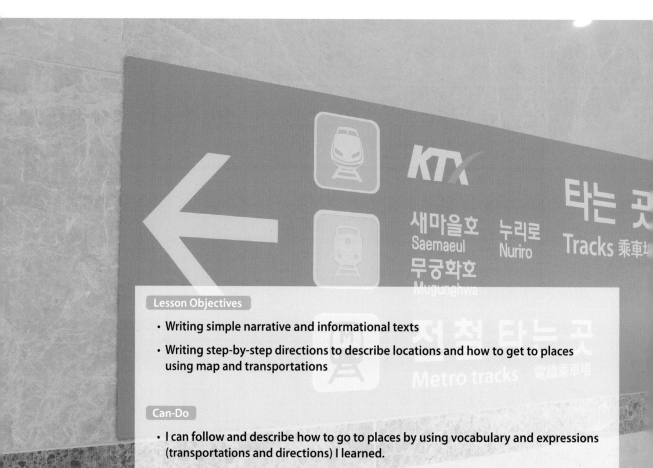

Lesson Objectives

- Writing simple narrative and informational texts
- Writing step-by-step directions to describe locations and how to get to places using map and transportations

Can-Do

- I can follow and describe how to go to places by using vocabulary and expressions (transportations and directions) I learned.
- I can ask for and provide simple directions using basic transitional words, phrases, expressions, and sentences.
- I can present simple information on locations of places and directions to places in simple sentences.

 ## Useful Vocabulary, Grammar, and Expressions

1. Vocabulary

(1) ☐ 자동차/차 car   ☐ 오토바이 motorcycle   ☐ 자전거 bicycle

☐ 택시 taxi   ☐ 버스 bus   ☐ 지하철 subway

☐ 배 boat/ship   ☐ 비행기 airplane   ☐ 기차 train

☐ 1호선 Subway Line 1   ☐ 출구 exit   ☐ 입구 entrance

☐ 지도 map   ☐ 노선도 route map   ☐ 버스 정류장 bus stop

☐ 역 station   ☐ 먼저 first   ☐ 그 다음에 and then

2. Grammar

① N(vehicle)(으)로 by N(vehicle)

② N(place)에서 N(vehicle)(으)로 갈아타다 to transfer to N(vehicle)at N(place)

③ N(vehicle)을/를 타다 to get on

④ N(place)에서 내리다 to get off

⑤ N(place)(으)로 나가다 to exit to N(place)

⑥ N(place)에서 N(place)까지 from N(place) to N(place)

⑦ N(time)이/가 걸리다 It takes N(time)

⑧ N(place)에서 떠나다/출발하다 depart from N(place)

⑨ N(place)에 도착(하다) arrive at N(place)

⑩ N(place)이/가 나와요/보여요/있어요. You will see N(place).

3. Expressions

① 걸어서 on foot

② 이쪽/그쪽/저쪽으로 가세요. Go this/that/over that way.

③ 어떻게 가요? How do I get there?

④ 얼마나 걸려요? How long does it take?

1. The following are directions that describe how to get to Kyungbok Palace (경복궁).

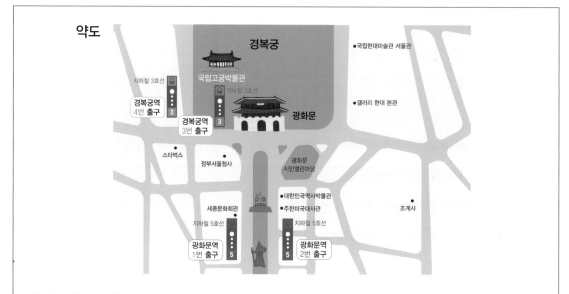

경복궁 찾아오시는 길

지하철 3호선을 타세요. 경복궁역에서 내리세요. 4번 출구로 나가세요. 걸어서 4분 걸립니다.

지하철 5호선을 타세요. 광화문역에서 내리세요. 1번 출구로 나가세요. 걸어서 2분 걸립니다.

약도 simple map, (찾아)오시는 길 How to get to this place

지하철 2호선 낙성대역

낙성대역 4번 출구로 나와서 똑바로 쭉 갑니다. 주유소에서 왼쪽으로 갑니다. 그럼 제과점이 나옵니다. 제과점 앞 정류장에서 마을버스 관악02를 타고 신공학관에서 내립니다.

지하철 2호선 서울대입구역

서울대입구역 3번 출구로 나와서 관악구청 방향으로 쭉 갑니다. 학교 셔틀 버스나 시내버스 5511 또는 5513을 타고 신공학관에서 내립니다.

지하철 2호선 신림역

신림역 3번 출구에서 나와 시내버스 5516을 타고 신공학관에서 내립니다.

(똑바로) 쭉 가다 to go straight, 왼쪽/오른쪽으로 가다 to go left/right, 방향(으로) toward, 또는/ ─(이)나 or, 신공학관 new engineering building, 제과점 bakery, 시내 버스 city bus

2. These are authentic directions on a Korean app. The app describes how to walk to Seoul Library (서울도서관) from Deoksu Palace (덕수궁) in Seoul.

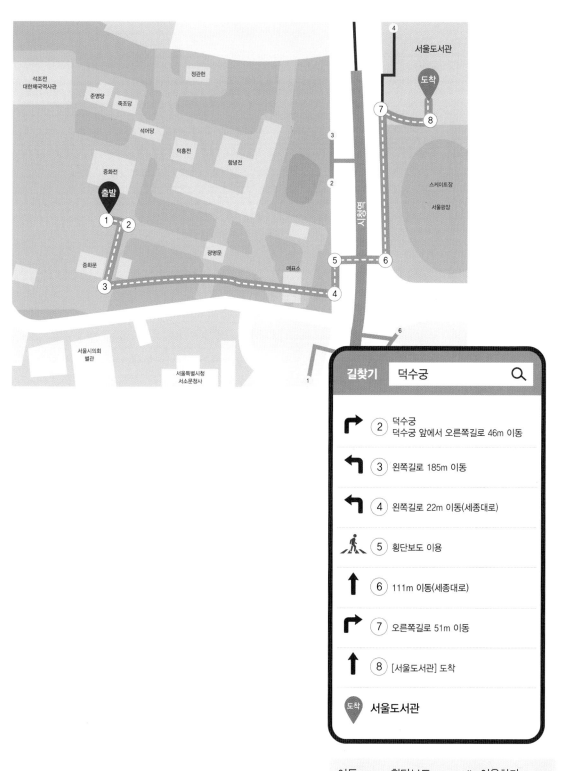

이동 move, 횡단보도 crosswalk, 이용하다 to use

1. What is the best way to get to the following places?

경복궁에서 인사동까지 걸어서 가요.

2. The following is a smartphone app's directions to Deoksu Palace (덕수궁) in Seoul, Korea. Rewrite the directions for a travel brochure.

먼저, 덕수궁 앞에서 오른쪽 길로 46미터 가세요.

그 다음에

3. Describe how to go to the places by subway, based on the Seoul Subway Route Map (서울 지하철 노선도).

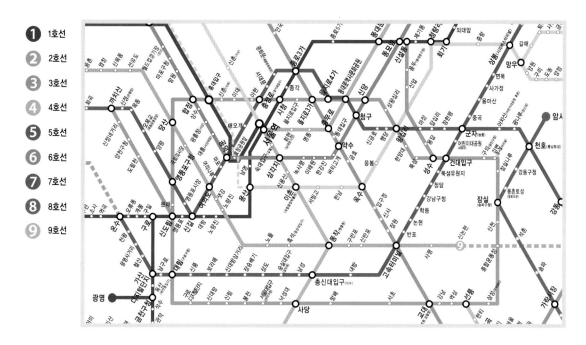

❶ 시청 → 국립중앙박물관

먼저, 시청역에서 1호선을 타세요. 그 다음에 서울역에서 4호선으로 갈아타세요.

이촌역에서 내리세요.

❷ 서울역 → 고속터미널

❸ 명동 → 이태원

❹ 홍대 입구 → 광화문

❺ 남대문 시장 → 압구정

4. You are at Insadong (인사동) in Seoul for a day tour. Based on the map, describe simple directions to the places you will stop by.

❶ 탑골공원 → 아름다운 차 박물관

탑골공원에서 나가세요. 그 다음에 왼쪽으로 가세요. 그럼 화장실이 보여요. 거기에서 오른쪽으로

쭉 가세요. 그럼 왼쪽에 아름다운 차 박물관이 있어요.

❷ 아름다운 차 박물관 → 경인 미술관

❸ 경인 미술관 → 조계사

❹ 조계사 → 보신각

❺ 보신각 → 서울 YMCA 관광호텔

Interpersonal Writing

1. You run a travel blog on social media. Your followers asked some questions about your recent post about your college. Reply to the questions.

❶ 안녕하세요. 저는 서울에 살고 있는데요, 이번 여름에 서울 대학교에 갈 거예요. 공항에서 학교까지

어떻게 가요?

❷ 학교 근처에 한국 식당이 있어요? 캠퍼스에서 어떻게 가요?

❸ 대학교 Visitor Center는 어디에 있어요? 감사합니다.

Presentational Writing

1. You work as a student tour guide for your school's Visitor Center. The Center is creating multilingual campus tour brochures for their increasing visitors from all over the world. So, your assigned task is to write directions in Korean.

   Write friendly and detailed directions to places on your campus in Korean. Include a campus map. Choose three campus places you will guide. Write walking directions to those places.

2. Introduce your favorite place on your campus including directions to that place.

Writing Tips

 길 안내에 쓰이는 문체

Sentence Ending Style for Giving Direction

When you write directions, it is common to end sentences with a noun to make the informative text more concise. You can give a lot of information clearly, and in a few words. Therefore, your direction is brief but comprehensive.

As in the authentic directions below provided on the Consulate General of the Republic of Korea website in Boston, each sentence ends with a noun. Those nouns are, in general, Sino-Korean words.

내리다 can be replaced with 하차; 타다 can be replaced with 탑승; 가다 can be replaced with 이동;

걸리다 can be replaced with 소요.

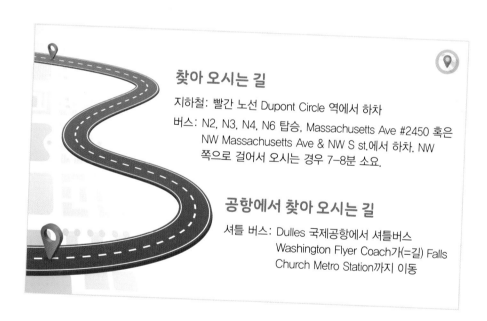

찾아 오시는 길

지하철: 빨간 노선 Dupont Circle 역에서 하차

버스: N2, N3, N4, N6 탑승, Massachusetts Ave #2450 혹은
NW Massachusetts Ave & NW S st.에서 하차. NW
쪽으로 걸어서 오시는 경우 7~8분 소요.

공항에서 찾아 오시는 길

셔틀 버스: Dulles 국제공항에서 셔틀버스
Washington Flyer Coach가(=길) Falls
Church Metro Station까지 이동

2.1. | 초대 Invitation

Lesson Objectives

- Writing simple text to invite someone to an event
- Writing to present and exchange informational text for an invitation

Can-Do

- I can identify key information on an invitation (e.g., when, where, why, etc.).
- I can exchange basic information in spontaneous communication about inviting people for events as well as replying to the invitation using practiced or memorized words, phrases, and simple sentences.
- I can present information on events (e.g. party invitation) and follow-up messages (e.g. thank-you note) using other visual modes (e.g. symbols, images).

 Useful Vocabulary, Grammar, and Expressions

1. Vocabulary

(1)
- ☐ 생일 birthday, 생신 birthday *(honorific)*
- ☐ 백일 100th day
- ☐ 돌 1st birthday
- ☐ 환갑 60th birthday
- ☐ 칠순 70th birthday
- ☐ 팔순 80th birthday
- ☐ 졸업 graduation
- ☐ 결혼 wedding
- ☐ 식 ceremony
- ☐ 집들이 housewarming
- ☐ 선물 present
- ☐ 꽃 flower

케이크 cake	떡 rice cake	초 candle
음식 food	음료수 beverage	과자 snack
과일 fruit	술 liquor	파티/잔치 party
친구 friend	손님 guest	초대 invitation
초대장 invitation card	날짜 date	시간 time
장소 place	준비물 things to bring	

(2)

초대하다 to invite	계획하다 to plan	축하하다 to congratulate
꾸미다/장식하다 to decorate	만들다 to make	사다 to buy
쇼핑하다 to do shopping	준비하다 to prepare	청소하다 to clean
주다 to give	받다 to receive	보내다 to send
사진(을) 찍다 to take photos	즐겁다 to be joyful	행복하다 to be happy

2. Grammar

① -아/어 주다/주시다/드리다 to do a favor

② -고 싶다/싶어 하다 want to

③ -아/어야 되다/하다 should

④ -(으)ㄹ게요 I will

⑤ -(으)ㄹ래요? Do you want to? / Shall we?

3. Expressions

① 축하해요/축하합니다/축하드려요/축하드립니다! Congratulations!

② 초대해 줘서/주셔서 고마워요/감사합니다. Thanks for inviting me.

1. Jenny is planning a surprise party for Minji's 20th birthday. She sent an e-card to Minji's friends to join the party.

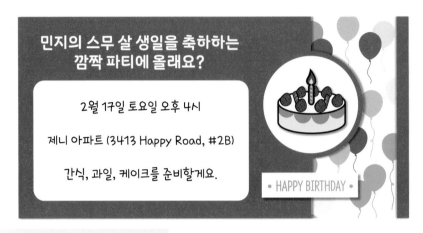

민지의 스무 살 생일을 축하하는
깜짝 파티에 올래요?

2월 17일 토요일 오후 4시

제니 아파트 (3413 Happy Road, #2B)

간식, 과일, 케이크를 준비할게요.

• HAPPY BIRTHDAY •

깜짝 파티 surprise party, 간식 snack, 과일 fruit

2. Jisoo received an invitation card to celebrate her grandmother's 70th birthday.

김정숙 님의 칠순 잔치에 여러분을 초대합니다

날짜: 9월 23일 금요일

시간: 저녁 7시-9시

장소: 서울 호텔 3층 가나다 홀

간단한 인사말 후에 저녁 식사가 시작됩니다. 시간을 꼭 지켜 주세요.
선물과 꽃은 받지 않습니다.
호텔 지하에 있는 주차장을 이용해 주세요.

님 Mr./Mrs./Ms. *(honorific)*, 여러분 all of you, 인사말 greetings, 식사 meal, 시작되다 to be started, 꼭 surely, 지키다 to keep, 지하 basement, 주차장 parking lot, 이용하다 to use

Pre-Writing Exercises

1. You are writing an invitation card for Susan's wedding reception party. Complete the message using suitable expressions such as -아/어 주다, -아/어야 하다, -고 싶다.

2월 23일 저녁 7시, 수잔의 결혼 축하 파티에

....! (오다)

장소는 수잔 집앞에 있는 공원 커뮤니티 센터(337 Happy

Road)입니다.

축하 영상에 넣을 메시지를 아래 .... (쓰다)

" .... "

파티에 올 수 있으면 이번 주말까지 저에게 .... (알리다)

함께 멋진 파티를 ....! (만들다)

(P.S.) 가능하면, 정장을 .... (입다)

그리고 선물은 수잔의 새집으로 미리 .... (보내다)

(주소: 777 Rainbow Drive, Wondertown, CA 93510)

장소 place, 아래 below, 가능하면 if possible, 미리 in advance, 주소 address

2. You received an e-card from Jason's roommates to celebrate his graduation and need to RSVP. Accept the invitation using suitable expressions such as -아/어 주다, -아/어야 하다, -고 싶다/싶어 하다.

졸업 축하 파티에 .... 감사합니다! 요즘 학기말이라서 좀

바쁘지만 꼭 ....

(제 룸메이트도 파티에 .... 괜찮아요?)

참, 제이슨이 .... 선물이 있어요?

그리고, 파티에 필요한 게 있으면 .... , 제가 사 ....

그럼, 파티에서 봐요!!! ^^

3. Reply to each text message appropriately.

① 준꼬

이번 주말에 제 룸메이트 생일 파티를 해요. 파티에 오실래요?

You

....

② 민지

다음 주 토요일이 아버지 생신인데... 무슨 선물이 좋을까요?

You

....

③ 마크

친구가 새집에 초대했는데... 한국에서는 집들이 때 보통 무슨 선물을 합니까?

You

....

④ 수잔

돌잔치에서 돌잡이 이벤트를 봤어요. 돈, 연필, 실이 있었는데... 무슨 뜻이에요?

You

....

돈 money, 연필 pencil, 실 thread

⑤ 가영

이번 여름에 졸업하지요? 축하해요! 선물로 뭐 받고 싶어요?

You

....

⑥ 데이빗

내년 봄에 저는 스테파니하고 결혼할 거예요! 저희 결혼식에 와 주시겠어요?

You

....

Interpersonal Writing

1. You and your friends in Korean class are planning a birthday party for your roommate Rachel who will turn 20 soon. The party will be held at 6 pm this Saturday in a community room at your apartment.

   (1) Write a group email to your friends (조앤, 마리아, 첼시, 앤디, 폴) who will help the preparation. Assign at least one thing for each friend using various endings (e.g., -아/어 주다, -(으)ㄹ래요, -(으)ㄹ게요).

보내는사람 _____

받는 사람 _____

제목 _____

여러분, 여기 레이첼 생일 파티 준비에 필요한 리스트가 있어요.

청소하기, 방 꾸미기, 시장 보기, 음식 만들기, 케이크 만들기, 선물/카드 사기

저는 ....

조앤 씨, ...

....

마리아 씨, ...

....

첼시 씨, ...

....

앤디 씨, ...

....

폴 씨, ...

....

아, 그리고 카드는 제가 ....

룸메이트 생일 파티를 도와 줘서 고마워요!!

---

(2) Write a birthday card to Rachel.

2. You are writing an eCard to Lawrence in order to ask him to join a Halloween Party. Complete the invitation with detailed information about the party.

3. Your friend Katherine invited you to her graduation concert this weekend, but you will be out of town and cannot join. Write a reply to say sorry and congratulate her graduation.

Presentational Writing

1. You recently moved to a new apartment in Seoul and plan to invite your colleagues at work to a housewarming party. Write an invitation card with information such as date/time and location.

2. Write a thank-you note to the people who came to your housewarming party.

Writing Tips

초대하기

Inviting people

Various expressions can be used to invite someone to an event. There is a slight difference in terms of nuance/politeness for each case.

ex 와 주세요 Please come to

와 주실래요/주시겠습니까? Will you come to

와 주시면 좋겠어요/좋겠습니다 It will be great if you can come to

초대합니다 I invite you to

참석해 주시면 감사하겠습니다 I will appreciate if you can attend

You can ask to RSVP using these expressions.

ex 오실 수 있는지 알려 주세요. Please let me know if you can come.

참석하실 수 있는지 알려 주시기 바랍니다. Please let me know if you can attend.

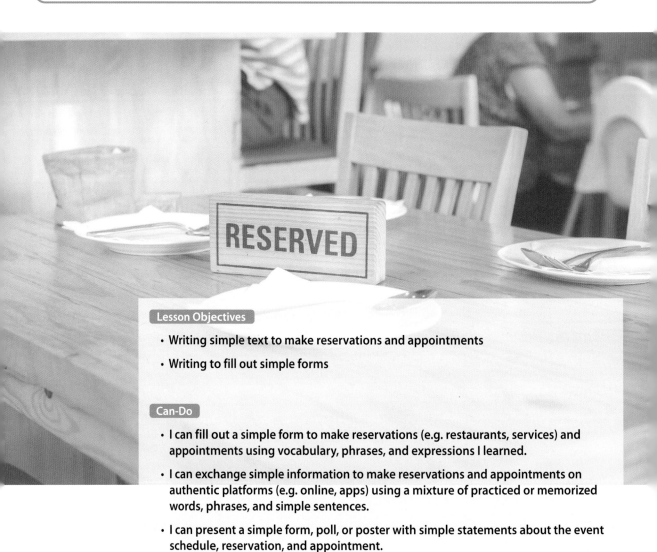

2.2. | 예약/약속 Making Reservations and Appointments

Lesson Objectives

• Writing simple text to make reservations and appointments

• Writing to fill out simple forms

Can-Do

• I can fill out a simple form to make reservations (e.g. restaurants, services) and appointments using vocabulary, phrases, and expressions I learned.

• I can exchange simple information to make reservations and appointments on authentic platforms (e.g. online, apps) using a mixture of practiced or memorized words, phrases, and simple sentences.

• I can present a simple form, poll, or poster with simple statements about the event schedule, reservation, and appointment.

Useful Vocabulary, Grammar, and Expressions

1. Vocabulary

(1) ☐ 시간 time   ☐ 날짜 date   ☐ 장소 place

  ☐ 주소 address   ☐ 연락처 contact information   ☐ 인원(수) number of people

  ☐ 목적 purpose   ☐ 이유 reason

(2) ☐ 예약하다 to reserve   ☐ 약속하다 to make an appointment   ☐ 취소하다 to cancel

☐ 상관 없다 It doesn't matter   ☐ 가능하다 to be possible   ☐ 알려주다 to inform/let someone know

☐ 물어보다 to ask/inquire   ☐ 여쭤보다 to ask/inquire (honorific)

(3) ☐ 아무 때나 at any time   ☐ 언제든지 whenever   ☐ 어디든지 wherever

☐ 뭐든지 whatever

2. Grammar

① -(으)려고 하다 to plan/intend to do something

② -아/어 주시면 감사하겠습니다 would appreciate if you kindly could

③ -(으)ㄹ 수 있다/없다 can/can't

④ -(으)ㄴ/는데요 (It is used to set background information)

⑤ -아/어 주시겠어요? Would you please?

⑥ N 빼고/말고 except for N

3. Expressions

① (저는) 좋아요. It is good (for me).

② 괜찮아요. It is ok.

③ 시간(이) 돼요. I'm available.

④ 죄송하지만, 시간(이) 안 돼요. Sorry, but I'm not available.

⑤ 그럼 그때/거기(에)서 뵙겠습니다/뵐게요. I will see you then/there. (honorific)

Writing Samples

1. Rina is ready to make a reservation for Kyungbok Palace (경복궁) Night Tour in Seoul, Korea. Refer to the information on the event poster to make a reservation online.

기간: 10월 1일 ~ 11월 30일

장소: 경복궁 (위치 보기)

관람 시간: 150분

나이: 전체 관람 가능

가격: 3,000원

예약 인원수: .... 명

예약하기

관람 visit (exhibition/tour), 야간 nighttime

2. Jackie is organizing a gathering event for the Graphic Design Club at Hankuk University. The event is open to all school community members, and you received the following invitation to schedule.

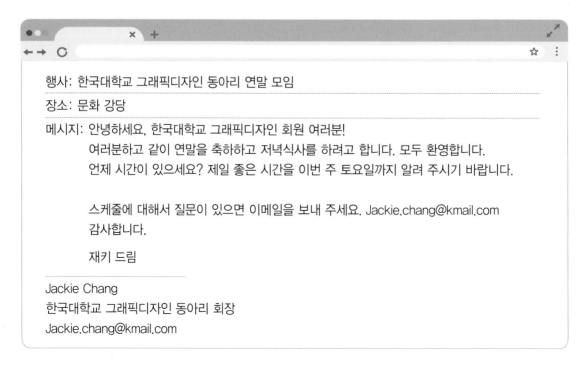

행사: 한국대학교 그래픽디자인 동아리 연말 모임

장소: 문화 강당

메시지: 안녕하세요, 한국대학교 그래픽디자인 회원 여러분!
여러분하고 같이 연말을 축하하고 저녁식사를 하려고 합니다. 모두 환영합니다.
언제 시간이 있으세요? 제일 좋은 시간을 이번 주 토요일까지 알려 주시기 바랍니다.

스케줄에 대해서 질문이 있으면 이메일을 보내 주세요. Jackie.chang@kmail.com
감사합니다.

재키 드림

Jackie Chang
한국대학교 그래픽디자인 동아리 회장
Jackie.chang@kmail.com

12월 9일 금요일			
	오후 5시~7시	오후 6시 30분~8시	오후 7시~8시 30분
캐씨 밀러	✔		✔
제이슨 박	✔	✔	✔
사무엘 소사			✔

행사 event, 모임 gathering, 연말 end-of-year

3. Samantha emailed her Korean TA to inquire if their meeting could be rescheduled.

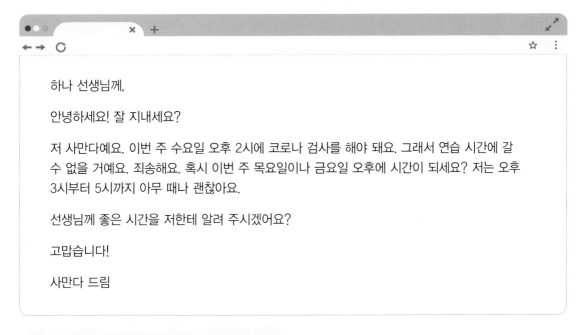

하나 선생님께,

안녕하세요! 잘 지내세요?

저 사만다예요. 이번 주 수요일 오후 2시에 코로나 검사를 해야 돼요. 그래서 연습 시간에 갈 수 없을 거예요. 죄송해요. 혹시 이번 주 목요일이나 금요일 오후에 시간이 되세요? 저는 오후 3시부터 5시까지 아무 때나 괜찮아요.

선생님께 좋은 시간을 저한테 알려 주시겠어요?

고맙습니다!

사만다 드림

혹시 by chance, 코로나 검사 COVID-19 test, 답장 reply

Pre-Writing Exercises

1. You and your friends are planning to eat at a restaurant. To make a reservation online, fill out the reservation form.

❶ 이름

❷ 연락처

❸ 이메일

❹ 예약 날짜

❺ 예약 인원수

❻ 예약 시간

2. You organize an event and collect information from the participants to determine the schedule. Create the event schedule form using a poll on a social media app.

스케줄 만들기 Scheduling Poll

(1) Write the event title, location, and a short message to the participants.

제목:

장소:

메시지:

(2) Provide the event time slots to choose.

날짜/요일/시간 (1): ....

날짜/요일/시간 (2): ....

날짜/요일/시간 (3): ....

(3) Put the event organizer's name and contact information.

이름: ....

이메일: ....

3. You are writing an email to your teacher to make an appointment. Write up your email inquiry to make an appointment following the step-by-step components.

❶ 받는 사람 : .... 께,

❷ 인사: ....

❸ 보낸 사람: ....

❹ 이유: .... -(으)ㄴ/는데요,

❺ 날짜, 시간: 혹시 .... 에 시간 되세요?

이 시간이 안 되면, 저는 .... 에도 괜찮습니다.

❻ 부탁: .... (으)면 감사하겠습니다.

❼ 인사: ....

❽ 보낸 사람 이름: .... 드림/올림

부탁 request

Interpersonal Writing

1. You are the secretary of your hobby club, and the club president requested you to make a restaurant reservation for a club gathering. Confirm the event with the club president by text messaging before making a reservation for the event. Ask and answer information about the possibility to make a reservation including 모임 목적, 시간, 장소, 날짜, 인원수, 인사, etc.

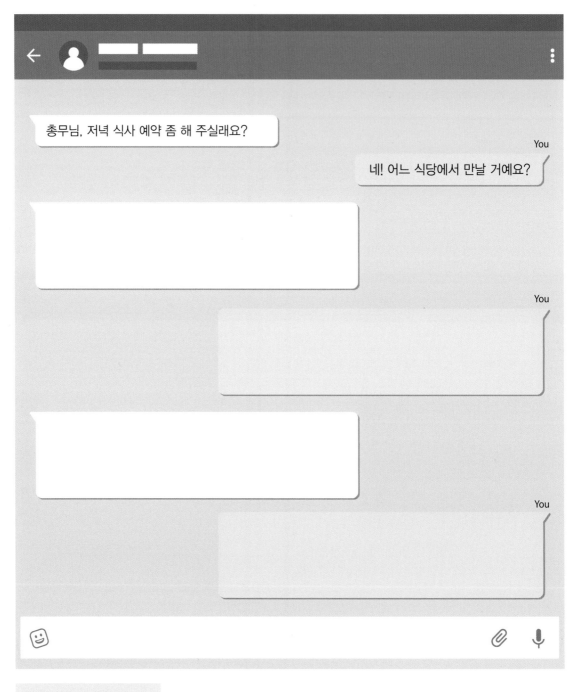

총무님, 저녁 식사 예약 좀 해 주실래요?

You
네! 어느 식당에서 만날 거예요?

You

You

회장 president, 총무 secretary

2. You are the cultural chair of your school's cultural organization and need to make a room reservation for its upcoming cultural performance show. Follow the direction and write an inquiry email providing information to the school's classroom reservation manager.

교실/강당 예약

예약 방법

1. 예약에 필요한 다음의 정보를 classrooms@Hankuk.ac.kr로 알려 주시기 바랍니다.

❶ 사용자/ 단체 이름: _____

❷ 연락처: _____

❸ 사용 목적: _____

❹ 인원수: _____

❺ 날짜 (년/월/일), 요일 _____

❻ 사용 시간: _____ 부터 _____ 까지

이메일을 보내 주시면 3일에서 5일 안에 답장을 보내 드리겠습니다.

감사합니다.

강당 auditorium, 단체 group/organization

_____

_____

_____

_____

_____

_____

Presentational Writing

1. You are writing an email inquiry to schedule a meeting with your professor. You cannot make your professor's offered office hours on the syllabus. In your email, include the following information: who you are, purpose, reason, your available times, asking for your professor's availability, appropriate greetings, etc.

2. You are going back home during the school break and seek a carpooler to the airport near your campus. Post your message for carpooling with some essential information about it to your school's online community site.

Writing Tips

 헷갈리는 맞춤법
Confusing Spelling

The following examples are commonly used in daily communication, but many people misspell them or get confused. Let's check the standard spelling of each word and use them properly for everyday writing.

❶ 메세지?　　메시지? (message)

❷ 스캐줄?　　스케줄?　　스캐쥴?　　스케쥴? (schedule)

❸ 알려 주시기 바래요?　　알려 주시기 바라요?

❹ 내일 뵐게요?　　내일 봴께요?

2.3. 동아리 가입 Joining Clubs

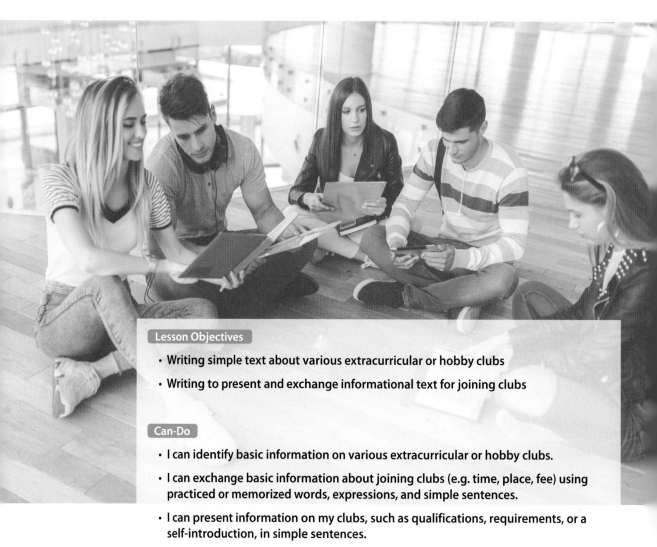

Lesson Objectives

- Writing simple text about various extracurricular or hobby clubs
- Writing to present and exchange informational text for joining clubs

Can-Do

- I can identify basic information on various extracurricular or hobby clubs.
- I can exchange basic information about joining clubs (e.g. time, place, fee) using practiced or memorized words, expressions, and simple sentences.
- I can present information on my clubs, such as qualifications, requirements, or a self-introduction, in simple sentences.

Useful Vocabulary, Grammar, and Expressions

1. Vocabulary

(1)
- ☐ 취미 hobby
- ☐ 특기 specialty
- ☐ 멤버/회원 member
- ☐ 동아리 extracurricular club
- ☐ 동호회 leisure club
- ☐ 동아리 방 club room
- ☐ 선배 senior
- ☐ 후배 junior
- ☐ 가입하다 to join
- ☐ 지원하다 to apply
- ☐ 모임 gathering
- ☐ 뒤풀이 after party

(2) ☐ 전혀 never   ☐ 가끔 sometimes   ☐ 보통 usually

  ☐ 자주 often   ☐ 매N(time)/N(time)마다 every N(time)   ☐ N(time)에 number 번 # times per N(time)

2. Grammar

① -아/어서 because, -기 때문에 because

② -(으)ㄹ 수 있다/없다 can/cannot, -(으)ㄹ 줄 알다/모르다 to know/not know how to

③ -(으)/ㄴ/는/-(으)ㄹ +N (Noun-modifying form)

3. Expressions

① 잘해요. I am good at it.

② 잘 못해요. I am not good at it.

③ 잘했어요! You did good!

④ 한번 해 보고 싶어요. I'd like to try it.

⑤ 환영해요/환영합니다! Welcome!

1. Natalie just moved to a new APT near college. She saw a flier on the APT bulletin board for recruiting new members of a coffee club.

"커피 마을"로 오세요!

커피를 사랑하고 즐기는 분,
커피에 대해 배우고 싶은 분,
모두 환영합니다!!!

정기 모임: 매주 수요일 오후 7시
장소: 아파트 1층 커뮤니티 센터 A100
준비물: 없음

모임 후 간단한 뒤풀이가 있습니다.

─에 대해 about, 정기 regular, 준비물 things to prepare, 후 after, 뒤풀이 after party

2. Jiwoo is interested in joining a saxophone club at her college. She wrote a self-introducing statement for the club application form.

안녕하세요? 저는 경제학과 1학년 윤지우입니다.

고등학교 입학 후에 색소폰을 배웠고, 4년 동안 학교 밴드를 했습니다.

저는 재즈 음악을 좋아해서 색소폰을 배우기 시작했습니다.

잘 하지는 못하지만 선배님들, 그리고 친구들과 같이 계속 연습하고 싶습니다.

경제학 Economics, 입학 entering school, 계속 continually, 연습하다 to practice

Pre-Writing Exercises

1. You are not sure which clubs to join at college. In order to make a decision, let's list three clubs you are interested in and the reasons to join.

ex 농구 클럽 : 운동을 자주 하고 싶어요. 그리고 팀 운동을 좋아해요.

❶ _____ : _____

❷ _____ : _____

❸ _____ : _____

2. You decided to join a ski club "FREE" and picked up its application form today. Let's fill it out with your information.

이름: _____

전공: _____ 학년: _____

전화번호: _____ 이메일: _____

지원 이유/목적: _____

_____

스키 실력: 초급 / 중급 / 고급

연습 가능 시간: 월 / 화 / 수 / 목 / 금 / 토 / 일

오전 / 오후

실력 skill, 초급 beginner level, 중급 intermediate level, 고급 advanced level, 가능 possibility

3. You are preparing for a club flier. Describe each club using a noun modifying form -(으)ㄴ/는.

ex 자연 친구

매주 일요일에 산이나 바다 등의 자연을 보러 다니는 동아리입니다.

❶ 두 바퀴

❷ 요리 조리

❸ 한글 사랑

❹ 춤춤춤

❺ 컴퓨터 놀이방

Interpersonal Writing

1. Company The ONE has been supporting various hobby clubs at work to encourage their employees. It is the Club Information Week to recruit new members this year.

(1) You went to an information meeting for a tennis club. Fill out the Q&A card with your questions about the club. You need information about the level requirement, practice day/ time, meeting place, membership fee, things to bring, competition schedule, etc.

Q 1. _____ ?

Q 2. _____ ?

Q 3. _____ ?

Q 4. _____ ?

Q 5. _____ ?

(2) A staff member of the tennis club gave you a flier with the basic club information. Based on it, write a memo for each question you had earlier. If anything is unclear, you can ask the staff for more details.

회사 동호회 "Love4T"

반: 초급, 중급, 고급   연습 시간: 매주 수요일 오후 6-8시

연습 장소: 회사 테니스장   회비: $10/월 (매년 시합 참가비는 회사에서 지원)

준비물: 라켓, 운동복 (공하고 물은 제공)

A 1. _____ .

A 2. _____ .

A 3. _____ .

A 4. _____ .

A 5. _____ .

지원 support, 제공 provide

Presentational Writing

1. You are an organizing staff for a hobby club at college and make advertising materials for the Open House Week for incoming students.

   (1) First, create a flyer introducing your club. (e.g. club name, time/place, requirements)

   (2) Based on the information above, write a presentation script introducing your club at the information session event.

2. You just joined a college, and the weekly newspaper of the school is updating its freshmen highlight section for its next issue, particularly focusing on their campuswide clubs. Write an article introducing your newly joined club.

   안녕하세요? 저는 .... 동아리 신입 회원입니다.

Writing Tips

신청서/지원서 쓰기 #1

Writing Application Forms #1

Here is the list of information you may need to provide for filling out forms in Korea.

1. **성명 (한글/영어/한자) name (Korean/English/Chinese)**

   `ex` 홍길동 / Hong, Gil-dong / 洪吉童

   ❶ Some forms request that you write your family name and given name separately, while others request that you write your full name together. For the latter case, write your family name first, then your given name.

   ❷ Most Korean names have three syllables where the first syllable is the family name and the following two syllables are the given name. No spacing is used between the family and the given names unless you have to clarify them.

   `ex` 황 보은 (last name: 황), 황보 은 (last name: 황보)

2. **성별 (남/여) gender (male/female)**

   `ex` 남

   Instead of the full word 남자/여자, only 남/여 is used in most forms.

3. **생년월일 date of birth**

   `ex` 2002년 9월 23일, 2002/09/23, 2002. 9. 23.

   Korean is a so-called macro-to-micro language. When you write a date in Korean, you need to start from a large unit to a small unit: year, month, day. Some forms use slash or period between the units.

4. **주민등록번호 resident registration number**

   `ex` 020923-1046916

   The most common ID card in Korea is 주민등록증 (resident registration card) which has a name, resident registration number, address, along with your photo. The resident registration number has a 000000-0000000 format: the first six numbers indicate the date of your birth (year, month, day). The latter seven numbers indicate gender (e.g. 1 for male and 2 for female) and hometown information.

5. **주소 address**

   `ex` 대한민국 경기도 고양시 일산구 주엽동 37-20

   Likewise, when you write an address in Korean, you need to start from a large unit to a small unit: country, province, city, district, street, street number

6. **연락처 (직장/자택/휴대폰/이메일) contact (work/home/cell phone/email)**

   `ex` 010-387-6307 / gildong@gmail.co.kr

   Currently, each cellphone starts with wireless service numbers (e.g. 010), then the remaining numbers are three/four digits and four digit combinations (e.g. 010-387-9750, 010-3892-5729). A landline number starts with region numbers (e.g. 02 for Seoul), then the remaining numbers are three/four digits and four digit combination (e.g. 02-387-9750).

2.4. 이메일/편지 Emails/Letters

Lesson Objectives

- Writing simple personal emails and letters
- Writing semi-formal interpersonal texts (e.g. emails/letters) in daily communication with people of different backgrounds (e.g. age, relationship)

Can-Do

- I can identify basic email/letter-writing related vocabulary, phrases, and expressions.
- I can use everyday and conventional email/letter writing format.
- I can send and reply to simple email messages and letters to teachers, colleagues, and friends in simple and loosely connected sentences.

 Useful Vocabulary, Grammar, and Expressions

1. Vocabulary

(1) Emails/letters

☐ 이메일/전자우편 email	☐ 편지 letter	☐ 보낸/보내는 사람 sender
☐ 받는 사람 receiver	☐ 제목 subject line	☐ 보내기 send
☐ 주소 address	☐ 답장 reply	☐ 전체 답장 reply all

- ☐ 확인 OK/Check
- ☐ 취소 cancel
- ☐ 지우기 delete
- ☐ 파일 첨부 file attachment
- ☐ 전달 forward
- ☐ 참조 CC (carbon copy)

(2) Addressing

- ☐ N(person)에게 To
- ☐ Name께 To *(honorific)*
- ☐ 씨/님 Mr/Mrs/Ms

(3) Sender signature

- ☐ N(person)(이/가/씀/보냄) From
- ☐ N(person) 드림/올림 From *(humble)*

2. Grammar

① -아/어 줘서/주셔서 고맙습니다/감사합니다 Thank you for doing

② -기를/-길 바라요/바랍니다 I hope that

③ -아/어 주시면 감사하겠습니다/감사드리겠습니다 I'd appreciate it if you'd do

3. Expressions

① 안녕하세요? Hello/Greetings, 안녕하십니까? Hello/Greetings *(formal)*

② 잘 지내세요? How are you? Are you doing ok?

③ 다름이 아니라, I'm contacting you because

④ 고맙습니다/감사합니다. Thank you.

⑤ 안녕히 가세요. Goodbye. *(Lit. Go in peace.)*, 안녕히 계세요. Goodbye. *(Lit. Stay in peace.)*

⑥ 건강하세요. Stay healthy.

⑦ 행복하시기를 바라요/바랍니다. I hope you are happy.

⑧ 그럼 또 연락드릴게요. Then I will contact you again.

⑨ 좋은 주말 보내세요. Have a good weekend.

Writing Samples

1. Sandra is a study abroad student in Korea and wrote a thank-you letter to the teacher at the end of the semester.

선생님께,

안녕하세요! 건강히 잘 지내세요?

이번 학기에 재미있고 친절하게 우리 수업을 잘 가르쳐 주셔서 감사합니다. 매일 매일 수업에서 많이 배우고, 친구들도 만나고, 한국어도 많이 배울 수 있었어요. 그리고 지난주에 선생님하고 반 친구들이 다 같이 경복궁에 갔을 때 너무 재미있었어요! 여기 같이 찍은 사진 한 장을 첨부합니다. 다시 한번 감사드립니다!

선생님, 방학 동안 건강하고 행복하게 보내시기 바랍니다. 그럼 다음 학기에 뵐게요. 안녕히 계세요.

산드라 올림

반 친구들 classmates, 학기 | semester

2. Alex is president of a student club and is writing an email to all members about the upcoming meeting.

받는 사람   hanwoori@mailman.com
제목   한우리 미팅
참조   alexshin@mailman.com
파일 첨부   회의.doc

보내기   취소

한우리 회원 여러분께

안녕하세요! 한우리 회장 알렉스입니다.

다름이 아니라, 다음 주 목요일 오후 3시–4시에 회의에 모두 와 주시면 감사하겠습니다. 첨부 파일에 회의 내용이 있습니다. 꼭 읽고 오시기 바랍니다.

그럼 곧 뵙겠습니다. 감사합니다.

알렉스 드림

회의 meeting, 내용 content, 곧 soon

Pre-Writing Exercises

1. You work for a Korean company. Your co-worker just sent an email to you, and you are replying to your co-worker. Put the corresponding words in a Korean email format.

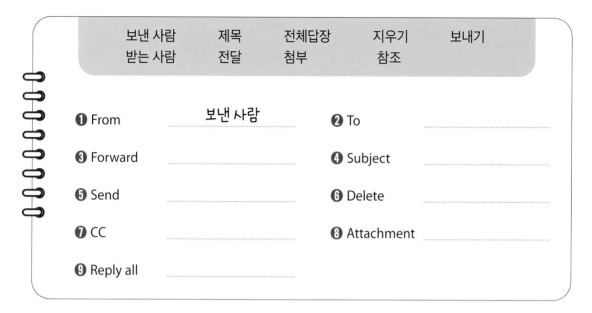

| 보낸 사람 | 제목 | 전체답장 | 지우기 | 보내기 |
| 받는 사람 | 전달 | 첨부 | 참조 | |

❶ From   보낸 사람   **❷** To

❸ Forward   **❹** Subject

❺ Send   **❻** Delete

❼ CC   **❽** Attachment

❾ Reply all

2. You are writing an email to your teacher to let them know of your absence from the class today. Complete the first draft by filling in the blanks and choosing the appropriate responses.

보내기   취소

❶ 받는 사람

❷ 제목

❸ _____ 에게 (   ) / 께 (   )

❹ _____ (Greetings)

❺ 다름이 아니라, 제가 오늘 _____ 아/어서 수업에 못 갔어요.

죄송합니다. 오늘 숙제를 _____ 면 감사하겠습니다.

❻ 그럼 내일 _____ 볼게요 (   ) / 뵐게요 (   ) / 뵐께요 (   )

❼ _____ 씀 (   ) / 드림 (   )

3. Kayla is interested in studying abroad in Korea to learn the Korean language and culture. She wrote an inquiry email to the staff in the Korean language program at Hankuk University about their summer session. Read her email and edit it appropriately before she sends it.

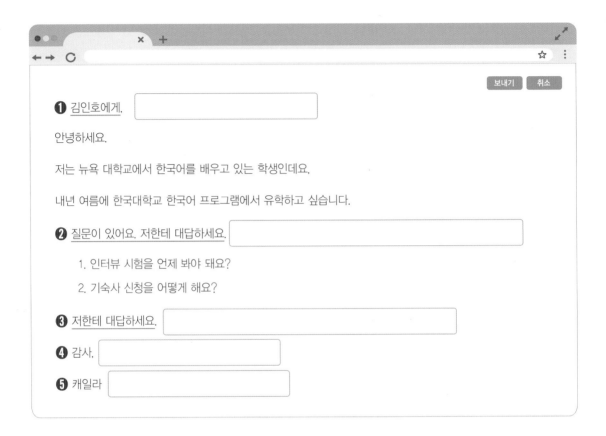

❶ 김인호에게,

안녕하세요.

저는 뉴욕 대학교에서 한국어를 배우고 있는 학생인데요.

내년 여름에 한국대학교 한국어 프로그램에서 유학하고 싶습니다.

❷ 질문이 있어요. 저한테 대답하세요.

    1. 인터뷰 시험을 언제 봐야 돼요?

    2. 기숙사 신청을 어떻게 해요?

❸ 저한테 대답하세요.

❹ 감사.

❺ 케일라

Interpersonal Writing

1. (1) You just found out that you cannot attend your class next week. Write an email to your teacher in advance to appropriately inform him/her of this.

(2) You have received an email from your student as in (1) above. Reply to your student.

Presentational Writing

1. You are a member of a fan club for your K-(Pop/Drama/Movie/Sports, etc.) Star. Write a fan letter to them.

2. The Wellbeing Center, your volunteering service in your local community, hosts a special event, *Letter to My (Future) Self*. You participate in this event and write a letter to yourself.

Writing Tips

 이메일/편지에 쓰는 호칭: 씨 vs. 님/선생님

Addressing Recipients in Email/Letter

When you meet someone for the first time or when addressing colleagues who are younger than you, you may address them [given name] / [family name + given name]+ 씨.

ex 예지 씨, 박예지 씨

However, [family name + given name]+님/ 선생님 is commonly used these days to show more respect, even though the addresses are not teachers.

ex 박예지 님, 박예지 선생님

 문장 부호: 쉼표 (,)

Punctuation Mark: Comma

에게/께 vs 에게/께,

In a letter or email written in English, it is conventional to use a comma (,) after the recipient's name.

ex Dear John,

In Korean letter writing, on the other hand, no comma is used in general.

ex 미류에게, 이 선생님께

 보낸 사람 이름 + 드림/올림

How to End an Email/Letter with your Name

When ending a letter, card, or email to colleagues, business-related people, or people older than you, write 드림 or 올림 after your name. 올림 is usually more formal and polite than 드림; however, 드림 is more commonly used among colleagues.

ex 홍지아 드림, 박윤수 올림

드림 is from 드리다 which means 'to send or give'. 올림 is from 올리다 which means 'to raise' (literally, you raise this letter to the receiver with both hands).

드림/올림 is used just as "with respect" or "sincerely yours" in English. For example, when you write to your parents, grandparents, teachers, 올림 is appropriate; when you write to your colleagues, business people, 드림 is commonly used.

2.5. | 물건 사기 Buying Things

Lesson Objectives

- Writing simple text for buying things
- Writing to present and exchange informational text about things to buy

Can-Do

- I can identify basic information on items to buy (e.g. ticket, clothing).
- I can exchange basic information about things to buy (e.g. price, quality) using practiced or memorized words, phrases, and simple sentences.
- I can present information on my shopping items (e.g. color, size, design, brand) through written and other visual modes (e.g. symbols, images).

 Useful Vocabulary, Grammar, and Expressions

1. Vocabulary

(1)
- ☐ 돈 money
- ☐ 현금 cash
- ☐ 신용 카드 credit card
- ☐ 값/가격 price
- ☐ 영수증 receipt
- ☐ 브랜드 brand
- ☐ 크기/사이즈 size
- ☐ 색(깔) color
- ☐ 모양 shape
- ☐ 무늬 pattern
- ☐ 디자인 design
- ☐ 길이 length

☐ 종류 kind	☐ 쇼핑하다 to do shopping	☐ 사다 to buy
☐ 팔다 to sell	☐ (돈을) 내다/지불하다 to pay	☐ 주문하다 to order
☐ 교환하다 to exchange	☐ 환불하다 to get refund	☐ 좋다 to be good
☐ 나쁘다 to be bad	☐ 크다 to be big	☐ 작다 to be small
☐ 맞다 to fit	☐ 길다 to be long	☐ 짧다 to be short
☐ 예쁘다 to be pretty	☐ 아름답다 to be beautiful	☐ 멋있다 to be cool
☐ 편하다 to be comfortable	☐ 불편하다 to be uncomfortable	☐ 어울리다 to fit; to match
☐ 싸다 to be cheap	☐ 비싸다 to be expensive	☐ 괜찮다 to be alright

(2) Color terms

☐ 빨간색 red	☐ 노란색 yellow	☐ 파란색 blue
☐ 보라(색) purple	☐ 하얀색/흰색 white	☐ 까만색/검은색 black
☐ 분홍(색) pink	☐ 주황(색) orange	☐ 연두(색) light green
☐ 초록(색)/녹색 green	☐ 하늘색 light blue	☐ 회색 gray
☐ 밤색 brown	☐ 금색 gold	☐ 은색 silver

(3) Question words

☐ 누구 who	☐ 언제 when	☐ 무엇/뭐 what
☐ 왜 why	☐ 어떻게 how	☐ 몇 how many
☐ 얼마 how much (price)	☐ 얼마나 how much (quantity)	☐ 무슨/어떤 what kind of
☐ 어느 which		

2. Grammar

① -아/어 보다 to try to

② -(으)려고 하다 to plan to

③ -(으)ㄴ 가요/나요? I am wondering if

3. Expressions

① 얼마예요?/얼마입니까?/얼마 해요? How much is it?

② 몇 달러/센트예요? How many dollars/cents is it?

③ 있어요/없어요? Do you have/not have it?

④ 현금으로/(신용)카드로 내 주세요. Please pay with cash/credit card

⑤ 싸게 해 주세요. Please make it cheaper.

⑥ 좀 깎아 주세요. Please give me a discount.

Writing Samples

1. Minji needs to buy an airline ticket to Korea for this summer vacation, but the Hankook Travel Agency in SF does not answer the phone. She instead leaves a text message.

> 안녕하세요?
> 여름방학에 한국 가는 비행기표를 사려고 합니다.
> 7월 5일 토요일에 샌프란시스코에서 떠나는 표가 있나요?
> 얼마예요? 그리고, 언제까지 사야 돼요?
> 510-387-6231로 전화해 주세요.
> 감사합니다.
>
> 김민지 드림

비행기표 airline ticket, 떠나다 to leave, −까지 until

2. Maria is collecting BTS photo cards. She saw an advertisement on the online buy/sell market and sent a text message to the seller.

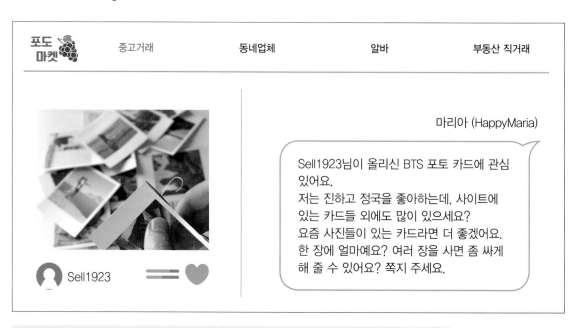

님 Mr./Mrs./Ms., 올리다 to upload, 포토 카드 photocard, 관심있다 to have interest, 외 other than, 요즘 recent, 장 piece, −(으)면 if, 여러 several, 싸게 cheaply, 쪽지 DM (direct message)

Pre-Writing Exercises

1. You need to buy a new computer. Send an email to your friend Mina who bought one recently and ask for its details. Also find out if she recommends getting the same computer.

(1) List the things you need to ask Mina.

브랜드, _____, _____, _____, _____, _____.

(2) Complete your email to Mina with suitable words and expressions.

받는 사람 ....

제목 ....

미나 씨, 얼마 전에 HP 컴퓨터 샀지요? 그거 ....? (How is it?)

비싸요? ....? (How much is it?)

.... 샀어요? (Where did you buy it?) .... 샀어요? (Did you buy it online?)

....? (Was it on sale?)

지난 번 컴퓨터보다 ....? (Is it faster?)

.... 좋아요? (What is good about it?)

저도 ....? (Should I buy the same one?)

2. You did grocery shopping online and just got the delivery. Out of seven items you ordered, one is missing, one is incorrect, and one is in bad condition. Fill out the complaint form to report to customer service and ask for a refund.

Items you ordered

우유 1병, 주스 2병, 버터 1개, 아보카도 3개, 치토스 과자 2개, 토마토 4개, 바나나 5개

Items you received

우유 1병, 주스 1병, 버터 1개, 아보카도 3개, 도리토스 과자 2개, 토마토 4개, 오래된 바나나 5개

이름	
연락처	
배달 날짜	
배달 주소	
배달 안 된 물건	
잘못 배달된 물건	
안 좋은 물건	

선택	다시 배달 ☐	환불 ☐	크레딧 ☐

다른 메시지	

배달 delivery, 선택 choice, 환불 refund

Interpersonal Writing

1. You often use an online shopping mall. Your favorite online shopping mall is e-WonderMall as it offers various items with good prices.

(1) You want to buy a pair of white, size 8, sneakers at the shopping mall. Fill out the instant chat conversation with a salesperson.

> **You**
> 신발 한 켤레 사려고 하는데요.

Salesperson
> 네, 어떤 종류가 필요하세요?

> **You**

Salesperson
> 원하는 브랜드가 있으세요?

> **You**

Salesperson
> 무슨 색이 좋으세요? 검정색, 파란색, 그리고 흰색이 있어요.

> **You**

Salesperson
> 사이즈는 어떻게 되세요?

> **You**

Salesperson
> 네, 그럼 오늘 택배로 보내 드릴게요. 아마 2-3일쯤 걸릴 거예요.

> **You**

Salesperson
> 저희 원더몰 사이트를 이용해 주셔서 감사합니다.

> **You**

(2) A few days later, you received the new pair of shoes but found out that the size is too small for you. Send an email message to the customer service and ask if you can exchange them with a bigger size.

서비스 센터 질문
Questions to Customer Service Center

You

(3) You received bigger size shoes today. You are very satisfied with the purchase and happy to fill out an online review form. Submit your customer review form.

이름	
구입 날짜	
구입 물건	
평가	아주 좋다 ☐　　좋다 ☐　　보통 ☐　　나쁘다 ☐　　아주 나쁘다 ☐
추가 의견	

구입 purchase, 평가 evaluation, 추가 additional

Presentational Writing

1. You got temporary housing near the summer internship company but it is unfurnished, so you need several used pieces of furniture (e.g. desk, chair, bed, sofa, lamp, drawer, closet). Write a posting to upload to the Buy & Sell e-bulletin board of the local community center. You can use expressions such as 구해요, -을/를 사고 싶어요, -이/가 필요해요.

2. You saw a moving sale advertisement on the Buy & Sell e-bulletin board of the local community center. Write to ask the owner about the furniture (e.g. price, state of items, and available date/time to pick up).

안녕하세요?

Writing Tips

금액 쓰기

Writing Amount of Money

The unit of Korean currency is 원(Won). There are no personal checks in Korea and only official checks issued by the Bank of Korea can be used. Below are the kinds of bills and coins that are currently used.

지폐 bill: 1000원, 5000원, 10000원, 50000원
동전 coin: 1원, 5원, 10원, 50원, 100원, 500원

Mostly, when numbers are written, there is a comma in the unit of thousand.

ex 1234567890 → 1,234,567,890

Also, there is a spacing in the unit of ten thousand.

ex 십이억v삼천사백오십육만v칠천팔백구십

However, in the case of the amount of money, you are allowed to write without the spacing to avoid any alteration. For the same reason, there is no spacing between the number and the classifier unlike other classifiers.

ex 십십이억삼천사백오십육만칠천팔백구십원

For the case of using Arabic numbers and classifiers, there is no spacing between them as in 100원.

수와 단위 명사 쓰기
Numbers + Counters

There are native Korean numbers and Sino-Korean numbers. You need to choose a number system along with an appropriate counter for each noun.

1. Only Korean numbers should be used for some counters.

   `ex` 달, 시

2. Only Sino-Korean numbers should be used for some counters.

   `ex` 년, 월, 일, 분, 초

3. Either Korean or Sino-Korean numbers can be used for some counters. In most cases, the Korean numbers are used for relatively small number of items while the Sino-Korean numbers are used for large number of items.

   `ex` 개, 명, 마리, 층, 장, 자루, 벌, 시간

Please note that different number systems can be used for different meaning.

   `ex` 이 권 (Vol. 2) vs 두 권 (two volumes), 오 과 (Lesson 5) vs 다섯 과 (five lessons)

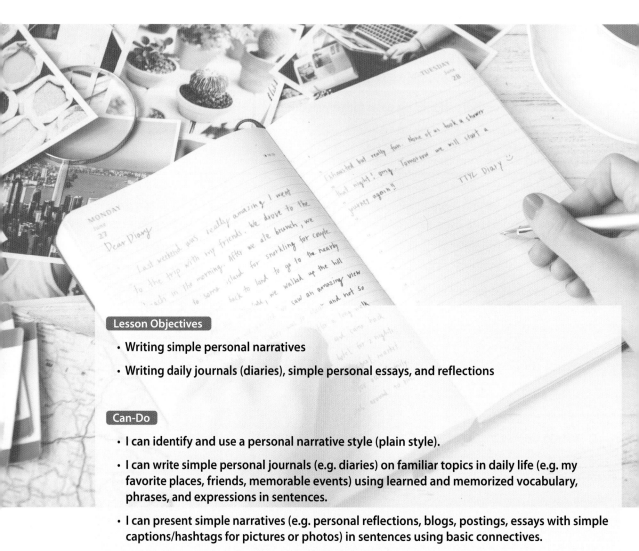

3.1. | 일기 Personal Daily Journal

Lesson Objectives

• Writing simple personal narratives
• Writing daily journals (diaries), simple personal essays, and reflections

Can-Do

• I can identify and use a personal narrative style (plain style).

• I can write simple personal journals (e.g. diaries) on familiar topics in daily life (e.g. my favorite places, friends, memorable events) using learned and memorized vocabulary, phrases, and expressions in sentences.

• I can present simple narratives (e.g. personal reflections, blogs, postings, essays with simple captions/hashtags for pictures or photos) in sentences using basic connectives.

Useful Vocabulary, Grammar, and Expressions

1. Vocabulary

(1) Daily journal writing

- ☐ 일기 diary
- ☐ 날짜 dates
- ☐ 요일 days of the week
- ☐ 날씨 weather
- ☐ 한 일 things (I) did
- ☐ 느낌 feelings

(2) Weather

- ☐ 맑다 to be clear
- ☐ 흐리다 to be cloudy
- ☐ 비(가) 오다 to rain
- ☐ 눈(이) 오다 to snow
- ☐ 바람(이) 불다 to be windy
- ☐ 따뜻하다 to be warm
- ☐ 시원하다 to be cool
- ☐ 덥다 to be hot
- ☐ 춥다 to be cold

(3) Seasons

- ☐ 봄 spring
- ☐ 여름 summer
- ☐ 가을 autumn
- ☐ 겨울 winter

(4) Feelings and emotions

- ☐ 기쁘다 to be pleased
- ☐ 행복하다 to be happy
- ☐ 기분이 좋다/나쁘다 to be in good/bad mood
- ☐ 슬프다 to be sad
- ☐ 화나다 to be mad
- ☐ 짜증나다 to be irritated
- ☐ 무섭다 to be scared
- ☐ 떨리다 to be nervous
- ☐ 걱정되다 to be worried
- ☐ 신나다 to be excited
- ☐ 외롭다 to be lonely
- ☐ 힘들다 to be hard/difficult/tired

2. Grammar

① 왜냐하면 -기 때문이다 because

② 그리고 and, 그런데/하지만 however/but, 게다가 in addition, 그래서 so/therefore

③ -(으)면서 to do A while doing B

④ -아/어도 even though

⑤ -(으)ㄹ 때(마다) when(ever)

⑥ -(ㄴ/는)다 Plain style: commonly used sentence ending in personal narrative/daily journal writing

3. Expressions

① 화이팅! Go! (a shout of encouragement or cheering)

② 비가 오나 눈이 오나 rain or shine

③ 기억에 남는 경험이에요. It's memorable experience for me.

Writing Samples

1. Adrian performed for the first time in the K-Dance Club at his school this weekend to showcase their new repertoire. After the show, Adrian posted his personal reflection to his social media group.

K-Dance 쇼!

오늘 우리 K-댄스쇼에서 처음으로 춤췄어요. 연습할 때 힘들고 어려웠어요. 하지만 댄스쇼 친구들하고 같이 할 수 있어서 행복하고 신났어요.

조금 떨렸어요. 그런데 많은 친구들이 우리 쇼를 보러 와 줘서 고마웠어요.

오늘 첫 공연을 잊을 수 없을 거예요. 우리 팀 화이팅!

#K-댄스 #행복 #잊을 수 없다 #첫공연

공연 performance, 힘들다 to be hard

2. Jenny wrote a personal journal about My Happy Place and published it in her school's multilingual journal club magazine.

나의 행복한 곳

제니 웬

나의 행복한 곳은 내 방이다.

내 방은 학교 기숙사에 있다. 우리 기숙사는 학생 회관 근처에 있다. 학생 회관에서 오른쪽으로 조금 걸어가면 길 건너편에 우리 기숙사가 있다. 내 방은 기숙사 3층에 있다.

나는 내 방이 크고 나 혼자 사용해서 참 좋다. 큰 방을 청소해야 돼도 내 방은 큰 창문도 있고, 창 밖에 예쁜 마당도 있고, 조용하다. 그래서 시간이 있을 때 방에서 책도 읽고, 컴퓨터에서 드라마도 본다. 나는 수업이 끝난 후에 보통 방에 와서 쉬거나 숙제하거나 공부한다. 자주 친구들하고 같이 방에서 얘기도 하고 K-POP 비디오도 함께 본다. 그래서 내 방에 있을 때 나는 스트레스가 없고 행복하다.

한 달 전에 나의 제일 친한 친구 한나하고 내 방에서 한국 영화 '부산행'을 같이 봤다. 영화를 보면서 치킨하고 떡볶이도 먹었다. 정말 재미있었다. 이번 주말에도 내 방에서 한나하고 영화를 볼 거다.

마당/정원 court yard, 사용하다 to use, 학생 회관 student center

Pre-Writing Exercises

1. You keep a diary. List how the weather was last week based on your daily journal.

비 ☂   눈 ❄   바람 ☁   흐림 ☁   맑음 ☀

❶ _____ 년 ____ 월 ____ 일 ____ 요일   날씨: **맑음**

❷ _____ 년 ____ 월 ____ 일 ____ 요일   날씨: _____

❸ _____ 년 ____ 월 ____ 일 ____ 요일   날씨: _____

❹ _____ 년 ____ 월 ____ 일 ____ 요일   날씨: _____

❺ _____ 년 ____ 월 ____ 일 ____ 요일   날씨: _____

2. Reflect on your week and describe your feelings and why. (Use -(ㄴ/는)다, the plain style.)

기쁘다 😊   힘들다 😵   신나다 😄   슬프다 😭

행복하다 😊   무섭다 ><   걱정되다 ☹

외롭다 ☹   기분이 좋다/나쁘다 😊😞   화나다 😠

❶ _____ -아/어서 **행복했** 다.

❷ _____ -아/어서 _____ 다.

❸ _____ -아/어서 _____ 다.

❹ _____ -아/어서 _____ 다.

❺ _____ -아/어서 _____ 다.

3. You are writing a highlight of your day and sharing it with your close friends on social media. Follow the guided process. You may use either -아/어요 or -(ㄴ/는)다 ending.

❶ Choose one highlight event that happened.

↓

❷ Write a draft of your post describing when, where, what, how, who, and why about the event.

↓

❸ Express your overall feelings about the event. You may use emojis to describe your feelings.

↓

❹ Add #hashtags (keywords) to your post.

↓

❺ Add a photo, image, or meme that captures your posting story.

Interpersonal Writing

- The Communication Chair of your community organization has contacted you to feature you in its special edition year-end newsletter. The Chair asked you to respond in writing to the interview prompts for the newsletter article. Respond to the following questions.

❶ '나의 행복한 곳'은 어디예요?

❷ 그곳은 어디에 있어요? 어떻게 가요?

❸ 그곳에서 보통 얼마나 시간을 보내요?

❹ 그곳에서 뭐를 할 수 있어요?

❺ 그곳에서 제일 기억에 남는 경험은 뭐예요?

기억에 남다 to be memorable, 경험 experience

Presentational Writing

1. You are living in Korea as a study abroad fellow. The fellowship foundation requires their fellows to post weekly highlights of fellow's journal blogs on their website. Post a short journal entry for this week, as you practiced in the Pre-Writing Exercises.

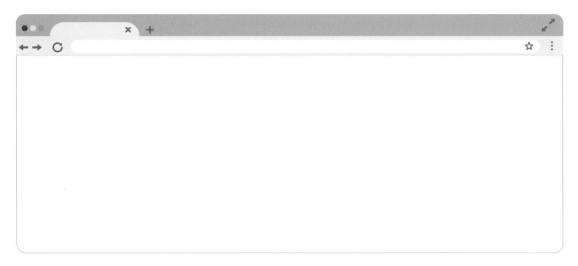

2. You are participating in a personal essay contest, hosted by the Korean Language and Culture Institute. This year, topics are:

   - My Precious Gift (나의 소중한 선물)
   - The Lucky Day (운 좋은 날)
   - My Best Friend Forever (BFF)

   Choose one topic and write your essay in sentences, including but not limited to:
   - What, Why, Where, How, Who, and When
   - Conjunctions
   - One major experience/storytelling
   - Your feelings

Writing Tips

–(ㄴ/는)다

Plain Style in Personal Narratives

When writing a personal narrative such as a journal or diary, the Plain Style is often used for sentence endings.

1. Present tense: verb stem + -ㄴ/는다 ; adjective stem + 다

   ex 요즘 나는 매일 걷는다.
   날씨가 흐리다.

2. Past tense: verb/adjective stem + -았/었다

   ex 오늘은 날씨가 좋았다.
   친구하고 점심을 먹었다.

3. Future tense: verb /adjective stem + -(으)ㄹ 거다

   ex 내일은 비가 올 거다.
   매일 걸을 거다.

4. N+(이)다

   이다 is used when a noun ends with a consonant and 다 when a noun ends with a vowel.

   ex 오늘은 일요일이다.
   그는 나의 친구다.

It is also correct to write 친구이다, and it is commonly used regardless of whether the noun ends with a consonant or vowel. However, 친구다 sounds more natural and appropriate both in speaking and writing.

저/제 vs 나/내

"I/My" in Plain Style

In plain style, first person subject in humble forms (i.e. 저/제) is not used. Instead, 나/내 is used.

   ex 나는 학생이다.
   저는 학생이다. (X)
   오늘은 내 생일이다.
   오늘은 제 생일이다. (X)

3.2. 축하와 감사 Congratulations and Gratitude

Lesson Objectives

- Writing simple text to express congratulations and gratitude
- Writing to present and exchange informational text about things to celebrate and appreciate

Can-Do

- I can identify basic and common words, phrases, and expressions in congratulatory and gratitude messages.
- I can exchange basic information in spontaneous written communication about things I want to celebrate and show gratitude using practiced or memorized words, phrases, and simple sentences.
- I can write to present simple congratulations and thank-you notes, card messages, or letters in sentences.

 Useful Vocabulary, Grammar, and Expressions

1. Vocabulary

(1)
- ☐ 생일/생신 birthday
- ☐ 합격 pass
- ☐ 입학 entering school
- ☐ 졸업 graduation
- ☐ 취직 getting a job
- ☐ 결혼 marriage
- ☐ 약혼 engagement
- ☐ 개업 opening of business
- ☐ 어버이날 Parents' Day
- ☐ 스승의 날 Teachers' Day
- ☐ 추천서 recommendation letter

☐ 올림/드림 from *(from a sender to a recipient who is older/higher)*

(2) ☐ 축하하다 to congratulate   ☐ 고맙다/감사하다 to thank   ☐ 태어나다 to be born

☐ 낳다 to give birth   ☐ 기르다 to raise   ☐ 되다 to become

☐ 좋다 to be good   ☐ 기쁘다 to be glad   ☐ 즐기다 to enjoy

☐ 행복하다 to be happy   ☐ 보내다/지내다 to spend time   ☐ 생각하다 to think

☐ 응원하다 to cheer   ☐ 바라다 to wish   ☐ 기대하다 to expect

☐ 돕다 to help

(3) Ordinal numbers: Korean number + 번째

☐ 첫 번째 1st   ☐ 두 번째 2nd   ☐ 세 번째 3rd

☐ 네 번째 4th   ☐ 다섯 번째 5th   ☐ 스무 번째 20th

☐ 스물 한 번째 21st

2. Grammar

① N(person/thing) +덕분에 thanks to N(person/thing)

② -아/어서 because, -아/어 줘서/주셔서 because you did it (for me)

③ -기를 바라요/바랍니다 hope to

④ -았/었으면 좋겠어요 It'll be great if

3. Expressions

① 축하해요/축하합니다/축하 드립니다! Congratulations!

② 잘됐어요! That sounds great!

③ 진심으로 감사 드려요/드립니다. I appreciate it from the bottom of my heart.

④ 행운을 빌어요/빕니다. I wish you a good luck.

⑤ (아주) 마음에 들어요. I like it (very much).

Writing Samples

1. Amy wrote a card for her best senior friend Jennifer who will graduate college this semester.

제니퍼 언니,

졸업 축하해요! 그리고 좋은 회사 취직도 축하해요!!

정말 정말 잘됐어요!!

그동안 멋진 선배가 돼 줘서 고맙습니다.

언니 덕분에 대학 생활이 편하고 재미있었어요.

자주 연락할게요. 사랑해요, 언니!!!

♥ 사랑하는 후배 에이미가

취직(하다) to get a job, 잘됐어요! Good for you!

2. Junko went to Alex's 1st birthday party last weekend and received a thank-you card from his parents today.

사랑하는 아들 알렉스의 돌 잔치에 와 주셔서

진심으로 감사 드립니다.

앞으로도 좋은 부모가 되기 위해 더욱 노력하겠습니다.

알렉스 아빠, 엄마 드림

앞으로 in the future, ―기 위해 for, 더욱 further, 노력하다 to do one's best

3. Choi's family sent a plant to celebrate the opening of 'Taste of Korea' in downtown.

축
개업

"한국의 맛" 오픈을 진심으로 축하 드려요.

식당이 잘 돼서 부~자 되시길 바랍니다.

스티브 가족 드림

부자 rich

Pre-Writing Exercises

1. You were accepted to a graduate school. Write an email to Professor Yoon who wrote a recommendation letter for you and share the happy news.

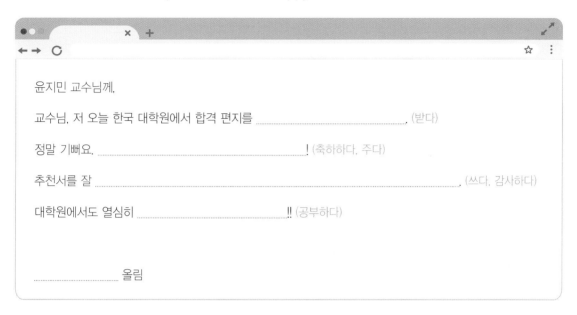

윤지민 교수님께,

교수님, 저 오늘 한국 대학원에서 합격 편지를 _____. (받다)

정말 기뻐요. _____! (축하하다, 주다)

추천서를 잘 _____. (쓰다, 감사하다)

대학원에서도 열심히 _____!! (공부하다)

_____ 올림

2. Last summer, you worked as a tutor for Mindy, who was a high school senior preparing for college applications. Today, you received an email from Mindy saying that she has been accepted to her dream school. Reply and wish her good luck.

민디,

와, 정말 반가운 소식이에요! _____! (축하하다)

민디가 열심히 _____ 이렇게 좋은 결과가 있었어요. (준비하다)

대학에서도 멋진 학생이 _____. (되다, 바라다)

행운을 _____! (빌다)

_____

추신: 참, 졸업도 미리 _____! (축하하다)

소식 news, 결과 result, 참 oh, 미리 in advance, 추신 P.S.

3. You are buying an e-Gift card for your cousin Woojin who is getting married next week. Write your message in Korean.

Gift card details						
Amount	$25	$50	$75	$100	$150	$200

Message

Quantity 1

우진 형/오빠,

드림

Interpersonal Writing

1. You got several text messages today. Respond to each text appropriately.

(1) Jeff and Paul sent you a couple of books for your 19th birthday. Reply to their text message in a group chat room.

제프 & 폴

> 열 아홉 번째 생일을 축하해요! 우리 책 선물이 마음에 들었으면 좋겠어요!
> 항상 좋은 친구가 돼 줘서 고마워요. 😊

(2) Mom also sent you a birthday present.

엄마

> 생일 축하해! 선물로 옷하고 신발 보냈어. 잘 맞아? 디자인은 어때?
> 운동 열심히 하고 건강하게 지내. 방학 때 보자.
> 사랑해~ 😍

(3) Your best friend Yumi is a good cook. As you've been sick this week, she made some Bulgogi and dropped it in front of your APT.

유미

> 주말에 불고기를 많이 만들었어요. 그래서 아파트 문 앞에 조금 놓고 왔어요.
> 맛있게 먹어요~~!!! 그리고 빨리 나아요!!!

낫다 to get well

1. May 8th is Parents' Day in Korea. Write a card/letter to your parents who live in Korea to celebrate Parents' Day and appreciate them.

사랑하는 아버지, 어머니께,

어머니, 아버지
고맙습니다
건강하세요

올림/드림

2. You are participating in a personal essay contest, hosted by the Korean Language and Culture Institute. This year's theme is "Dear My Teacher," aimed at expressing your gratitude on Teachers' Day.

선생님께,

스승의은혜
감사합니다

년   월   일

올림/드림

Writing Tips

 생일 축하 인사 쓰기
"Happy Birthday" in Writing

축 생일!!!

생일 축하해!!!

생일 축하해요!!!

생일 축하합니다!!!

생신 축하드려요!!!

생신 축하드립니다!!!

There are various ways to express "Happy birthday!" in writing depending on the relationships between a writer and a reader. For someone who is a peer or younger than you, 생일 and 축하하다 can be used. You can use 생신 and 축하드리다 for someone who is older and/or higher in social position than you to be more polite.

 헷갈리는 맞춤법: "되다" vs "돼다"
Confusing Spelling: "to become"

되다 is a word that even native speakers sometimes make spelling mistakes. Please note that 되 becomes 돼 only when it conjugates with 어 such as follows.

ex 되+어요 → 돼요

돼서, 됐어요, 됐고, 됐으면, 됐으니까, 됐지만

Remember that it does not change otherwise.

ex 됩니다, 되고, 되면, 되니까, 되지만

거절과 사과 Refusals and Apologies

Lesson Objectives

- Writing simple text to refuse or apologize
- Writing to present or exchange simple refusals/apologies politely

Can-Do

- I can recognize and apply basic writing conventions of refusing and apologizing.
- I can reply to others to decline (simple invitations, offers, or requests) and apologize in familiar everyday situations using highly practiced words and expressions in simple sentences.
- I can present, in writing, refusals by applying culturally appropriate communication strategies (e.g. thanking, explaining, indirect expressions) in simple and loosely connected sentences.

 Useful Vocabulary, Grammar, and Expressions

1. Vocabulary

(1) ☐ 먼저 first of all ☐ 갑자기 suddenly, unexpectedly

(2) ☐ 정말/진짜 really ☐ 너무/대단히 very, considerably

2. Grammar

① -아/어서 죄송해요/죄송합니다/ 미안해요/미안합니다 sorry for

② -(으)려고 했지만 I intended to do but/I was going to do but

③ -아/어야 되다/하다 should/have to

④ -고 싶은데/싶지만 I'd love/like to but

⑤ 못 -(으)ㄹ 것 같다 / -(으)ㄹ 수 없을 것 같다 I don't think that I can/I'm afraid that

⑥ -아/어서요 It is because

⑦ -아/어 줘서/주셔서 고마워요/감사합니다 Thank you for

⑧ -기(를) 바라요/바랍니다 I wish that

3. Expressions

① 무엇보다(도) most of all, 다시 한번 once again, 사실은 to tell the truth, 아쉽게도 unfortunately, 다음에 next time

② 이해해 주셔서 감사합니다. Thank you for your understanding.

③ 다른 일이 있어요. I have other plans.

④ 급한 일이 생겼어요. I have an urgent matter.

⑤ 글쎄요… Well…/I'm not sure/I don't know…

⑥ 생각해 볼게요/보겠습니다. I'll think about it.

⑦ 알려 드릴게요/드리겠습니다. I'll let you know.

1. Yeji is a college student in the U.S. It is Friday night, and Yeji got a text message about her favorite K-pop singer Hannie's online concert from her friend in Korea. The show will start tomorrow morning (Eastern U.S. Time) / night (Korea Time), and Yeji has a time conflict. So, Yeji is declining the invitation.

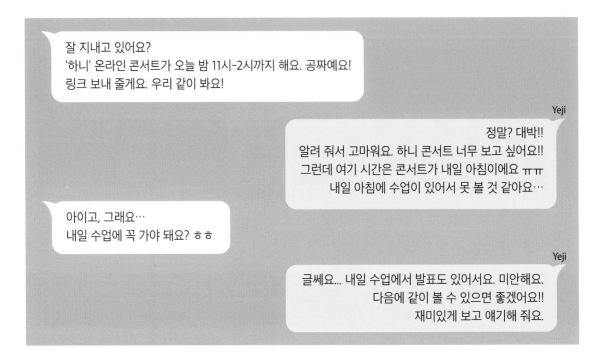

잘 지내고 있어요?
'하니' 온라인 콘서트가 오늘 밤 11시-2시까지 해요. 공짜예요!
링크 보내 줄게요. 우리 같이 봐요!

Yeji

정말? 대박!!
알려 줘서 고마워요. 하니 콘서트 너무 보고 싶어요!!
그런데 여기 시간은 콘서트가 내일 아침이에요 ㅠㅠ
내일 아침에 수업이 있어서 못 볼 것 같아요…

아이고, 그래요…
내일 수업에 꼭 가야 돼요? ㅎㅎ

Yeji

글쎄요... 내일 수업에서 발표도 있어서요. 미안해요.
다음에 같이 볼 수 있으면 좋겠어요!!
재미있게 보고 얘기해 줘요.

2. Jose is a college student in Korea, and one of his professors sent him an email to ask if he is interested in a part-time job position. The following is Jose's reply to the professor.

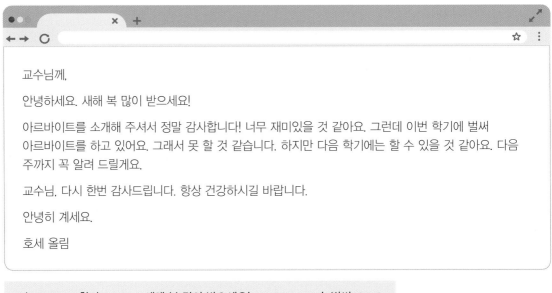

교수님께,

안녕하세요. 새해 복 많이 받으세요!

아르바이트를 소개해 주셔서 정말 감사합니다! 너무 재미있을 것 같아요. 그런데 이번 학기에 벌써 아르바이트를 하고 있어요. 그래서 못 할 것 같습니다. 하지만 다음 학기에는 할 수 있을 것 같아요. 다음 주까지 꼭 알려 드릴게요.

교수님, 다시 한번 감사드립니다. 항상 건강하시길 바랍니다.

안녕히 계세요.

호세 올림

교수 professor, 학기 semester, 새해 복 많이 받으세요! Happy New Year!, 벌써 already

Pre-Writing Exercises

1. You just found out that you can't join the group lunch with your Korean class today. Text in the group chat room to let them know and express your apology. Write your text message choosing useful words, phrases, and expressions given in the guided steps.

(1) An expression of an apology

미안하다, 죄송하다, 정말, 너무, 진짜 …

(2) Main message

못, -(으)ㄹ 수 없는데요, -(으)ㄹ 것 같아요 …

(3) Giving a reason/explanation/account

-(아/어)서요, -(아/어)야 돼서요 …

(4) Closing

-(으)세요, -기 바라요 …

2. Your colleague sent you and other colleagues in the office an email invitation for a K-BBQ picnic at a park, scheduled for the week after next Saturday at noon. Reply to your colleague to inform your refusal appropriately following the guided process with the helpful words and phrases suggested.

(1) Pre-refusal such as acknowledgment, willingness, wishes

먼저, −(아/어) 주셔서 감사합니다, −고 싶다, −(으)면 좋겠다 …

(2) Main refusal

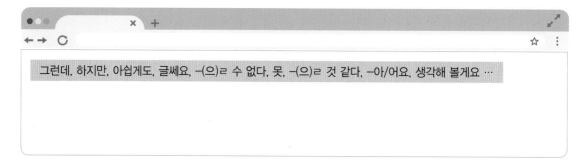

그런데, 하지만, 아쉽게도, 글쎄요, −(으)ㄹ 수 없다, 못, −(으)ㄹ 것 같다, −아/어요, 생각해 볼게요 …

(3) Post-refusal such as apology, reason, excuse

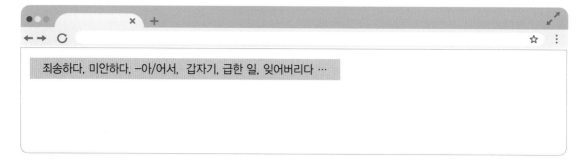

죄송하다, 미안하다, −아/어서, 갑자기, 급한 일, 잊어버리다 …

(4) Closing such as greeting, offer

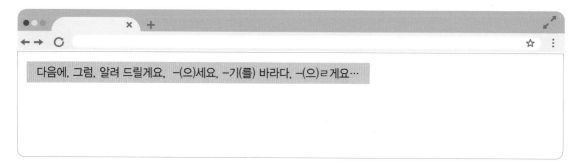

다음에, 그럼, 알려 드릴게요, −(으)세요, −기(를) 바라다, −(으)ㄹ게요…

Interpersonal Writing

1. Jaselene, one of your school club members, sent you a text message to invite you. Read the message and respond with your refusal by applying the guided process you just practiced.

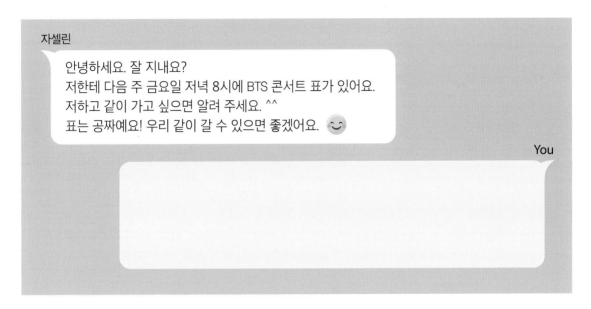

자셀린

안녕하세요. 잘 지내요?
저한테 다음 주 금요일 저녁 8시에 BTS 콘서트 표가 있어요.
저하고 같이 가고 싶으면 알려 주세요. ^^
표는 공짜예요! 우리 같이 갈 수 있으면 좋겠어요. 😊

You

2. Your roommate, Austin, just sent you an instant message, and you just realized that it was your turn to take the trash out to the apartment dumpster this morning. Write your response applying the guided process as in the pre-writing exercises.

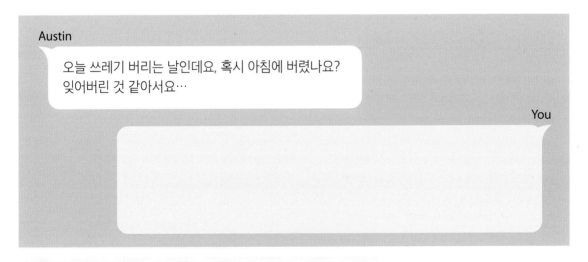

Austin

오늘 쓰레기 버리는 날인데요, 혹시 아침에 버렸나요?
잊어버린 것 같아서요…

You

쓰레기 trash, 버리다 to take out (trash), throw away, 혹시 −나요? Perhaps −?

1. You received a study abroad fellowship that allows you to go to Korea next summer. But unfortunately, you cannot go to Korea next summer. Write a turn-down letter with your sincere apology.

   Guided process:
   - Writing a letter (Refer to Lesson 2.4.)
   - Apologizing and Declining

     - Pre-refusal (e.g. greetings, acknowledgment)
     - Main Refusal (e.g. turning down the offer, fellowship)
     - Apology (e.g. apology, reason, explanation)
     - Closing (e.g. greetings, wishes for the addressee)

2. This year, the Korean Cultural Center is hosting a writing contest about the Korean traditional folktale story, 'Golden Ax, Silver Ax.' Enter your writing for the chance to win $500 and your story's publication on its website.

   Writing Contest Prompt:

   Read a part of 'Golden Ax, Silver Ax', a Korean folktale below and write an apology letter in Korean, as the greedy woodcutter, to the mountain god.

   > 옛날 옛날에, 비싼 은도끼와 금도끼를 원한 욕심 많은 나무꾼이 있었어요. 그래서 나무꾼은 숲속에 있는 연못에 갔어요. 그리고 그의 낡은 도끼를 일부러 연못에 던지고 산신령님이 나오기를 기다렸어요.
   >
   > 산신령님이 연못에서 나와서 나무꾼에게 말했어요. "너는 왜 울고 있니?"
   >
   > 욕심쟁이 나무꾼은 대답했어요. "제 도끼를 잃어버렸어요. 제 도끼가 없으면 저는 일할 수 없어요! 어떡해요?"
   >
   > 산신령님은 말했어요. "그래, 너의 도끼를 찾아줄게. 여기서 잠깐 기다려."

산신령님은 연못으로 들어갔어요. 그리고 잠시 후에 금도끼와 은도끼를 가지고 돌아왔어요.

"이 금도끼가 네 것이니?"

나무꾼이 말했어요. "네, 신령님, 제 도끼예요. 그리고 은도끼도 제 거예요."

산신령님은 화가 나서 소리쳤어요. "왜 거짓말을 하고 있어? 너는 아주 정직하지 않은 나쁜 사람이구나.

거짓말을 했으니까 벌을 받을 거야! 여기서 나가!"

"아이고, 산신령님!, 용서해 주세요."

하지만 산신령님은 연못 안으로 도끼들을 가지고 들어갔어요.

욕심쟁이 나무꾼이 하루 종일 산신령님을 기다렸지만 신령님은 돌아오지 않았어요. 욕심쟁이 나무꾼은 자기의 쇠도끼뿐만 아니라 금도끼와 은도끼도 다 잃었어요.

A long, long time ago, there was a greedy woodcutter who wanted expensive silver and golden axes for himself, so he went to the pond in the mountain forest. He dropped his old ax into the pond on purpose and waited for the mountain god to appear, crying loudly.

As expected, the mountain god appeared from the pond and asked the greedy woodcutter, "Why are you crying?" The greedy woodcutter replied, "I lost my ax, and I can't work without it! What shall I do?" After hearing this, the mountain god said, "I see. I will find your ax. Just wait here." The mountain god disappeared into the pond.

A moment later, he reemerged. He was holding silver and golden axes in his hands. He asked the greedy woodcutter, "Is this golden ax yours?" The greedy woodcutter said "Yes, Mountain God, that's my ax. The silver ax is mine as well!"

When he heard this, the mountain god shouted angrily, "Why are you telling lies? You're a bad and dishonest man. You will be punished for your lies! Be gone!"

"Oh! Mountain god, please forgive me."

But the god disappeared into the pond with the axes. The greedy woodcutter waited for the mountain god all day long, but the god never came back. The greedy woodcutter not only lost the golden and silver axes, but he lost his own iron ax as well.

신령님 mountain god, 나무꾼 woodcutter, 도끼 ax, 금 gold, 은 silver, 쇠 iron, 욕심(을) 부리다 to be greedy, 거짓말(을) 하다, to lie, 잘못 fault, 용서하다 to forgive, 정직하다 to be honest

---

신령님께,

욕심 많은 나무꾼 _____ 올림

간접 표현 #1
Indirect Expressions and Politeness #1

It is generally considered that moderate indirectness, although it may sound weak, is better and more easily acceptable than blunt and direct language among close friends and other acquaintances in everyday verbal and written communication.

> ex 안 가요. > 갈 수 없어요. > 갈 수 없을 것 같아요.

헷갈리는 띄어쓰기: 한 번 vs 한번
Confusing Spacing

한 번, 두 번, 세 번… means one time, two times, three times…etc. emphasizing the number of times. 한번 without space in between means "just" and does not emphasize the number.

> ex 한국에 한 번 가 봤어요. I visited Korea one time.
> 한국에 한번 가 보세요. Just try to visit Korea.

If 한 번 can be replaced with 두 번, 세 번… etc. in the context, there is space between 한 and 번 (한 번), and if not, then it is spelled as one word (한번).

> ex 다시 한번?/ 한 번? 감사드립니다. Once again, thank you very much.

In this case, 다시 한 번/ 두 번/세 번… 감사드립니다. 한번 cannot be replaced with 두 번, 세 번…etc.. Therefore, 한번 is the correct one.

거절문/사과문 쓰기
Writing a Refusal and Apology

Knowing how to apologize and refuse effectively and sincerely is crucial in written communication. However, since writing is expressed only in the written language without gestures, voice tone, intonation, facial expressions, attitude, etc., the good use of appropriate language expression is inevitably more critical.

The first step in writing an apology letter is to tell the reader what the letter is about. You may want to start your first sentence with explaining what you did wrong and acknowledge the consequences of your mistakes.

A sincere apology would include saying "I'm sorry" without excuses or blaming other factors. When writing a letter of refusal, it is usual to begin by thanking the reader for their offer.

Here is a summary of valuable tips you learned in this lesson:

1. Use polite language: In Korean culture, it's important to use polite language when apologizing or refusing. This shows respect and humility. Make sure to use the appropriate level of formality depending on the relationship and situation.

2. Be sincere: When apologizing, be sincere in your words and tone. Express your regret and take responsibility for your actions. When refusing, explain your reasons clearly and respectfully.

3. Use honorifics: When apologizing or refusing to someone (older or of higher social status, colleagues, in business), it's common to use honorifics to show respect. It is command to use "-습니다" or "-요" at the end of your sentences to convey this.

4. Offer a solution: When apologizing, offer a solution to make things right. When refusing, suggest an alternative or compromise if possible.

5. Use common expressions for apologizing and refusing in Korean, as shown in this lesson.

Overall, showing humility, sincerity, and respect through your language can go a long way in conveying your apology or refusal in Korean.

3.4. 양식 작성 Filling-out Forms

Lesson Objectives

- Writing simple text to fill out a form
- Writing to present and exchange basic information to fill out simple forms

Can-Do

- I can identify basic information in various simple forms.
- I can exchange basic information about things I need to fill out (e.g. club/ID card, part-time job application form) using practiced or memorized words, phrases, and simple sentences.
- I can provide my personal information and other relevant background required in authentic and familiar forms.

 Useful Vocabulary, Grammar, and Expressions

1. Vocabulary

(1)
- ☐ 이름/성명 name
- ☐ 나이 age
- ☐ 성별 gender
- ☐ 남 male
- ☐ 여 female
- ☐ 연락처 contact information
- ☐ 주소 address
- ☐ 전자우편/이메일 email
- ☐ 전화번호 phone number
- ☐ 휴대전화/휴대폰 cellphone
- ☐ 가족 관계 family relationship
- ☐ 주민등록번호 resident registration number

☐ 학력 educational background　　☐ 경력 work experience　　☐ 학생증 student ID

☐ (운전) 면허증 (driver's) license　　☐ 자격증 certificate　　☐ 경험 experience

☐ 취미 hobby　　☐ 특기 specialty　　☐ 양식 form

☐ 서류 document　　☐ 신청서/가입서/지원서 application form　　☐ 이력서 resume

☐ 자기 소개서 self-introduction　　☐ 추천서 recommendation letter　　☐ 비밀번호 password

☐ 대문자 capital letter　　☐ 소문자 lowercase letter　　☐ 숫자 number

☐ 부호 symbol

(2) ☐ 쓰다 to write/use　　☐ 사용하다/이용하다 to use　　☐ 신청하다 to apply/sign up

☐ 가입하다 to join　　☐ 지원하다 to apply　　☐ 작성하다 to fill out

☐ 내다/제출하다 to submit　　☐ 남기다 to leave

2. Grammar

① -아/어 주세요/주십시오 Please do (for me)

3. Expressions

① 어떻게 도와 드릴까요? How can I help you?

② 우선 이 양식을 써/작성해 주세요/주십시오. First, please fill out this form.

③ 연락처를 남겨 주세요. Please leave your contact information.

④ 곧 연락 드리겠습니다. I will contact you soon.

⑤ 동의합니다. I agree.

⑥ 회원 가입이 (완료)됐습니다. Your membership application is completed.

1. Minji, a freshman at Hankook University in Korea, is applying for a student I.D.

학생증 신청서

성명: (한글) 김민지 (영어) Kim, Minji (한자) 金旼祉

학번: 25692-7430

학과: 경제학 학년: 1

주소: 서울특별시 은평구 갈현동 37

전화번호: 02-398-6492

이메일: minji@hankook.ac.kr

2. Soomi is applying for a web designer position at Aram Publishing Company.

(1) First, she filled out a job application.

입사 지원서

지원 회사 아람 출판사 **지원 분야** 웹 디자이너 (정규직)

기본 정보

이름: 윤수미 (Yoon, Soomi)
성별: 여
휴대폰: 010-123-4567
이메일: soomi0923@gmail.com
주소: 서울 특별시 강남구 압구정동 현대 아파트 7동 509호
홈페이지: http://www.soomi.co.kr

학력

2023. 03 - 2027. 02	한국대학교 디자인학과	실용 미술 전공 (학점 3.9/4.0)
2025. 09 - 2026. 06	프랑스 파리 디자인 학교	교환학생(학점 4.0/4.0)
2020. 03 - 2023. 2	서울 여자 고등학교	
2017. 03 - 2020. 02	서울 여자 중학교	

경력 및 수상

2027. 01	제 15회 대한민국 디자인 공모전	대상 (실용 디자인 부분)
2026. 09 - 2027. 02	한국대학교 디자인학과	조교 (정시우 교수님)
2026. 06 - 2026. 08	디자인 하우스	디자이너 (인턴)
2024. 10	서울시 홍보팀	홍보 디자인 자원봉사

입사 지원서 job application, 출판사 publishing company, 분야 field, 정보 information, 학력 academic background, 실용 미술 practical art, 교환 학생 exchange student, 경력 job experience, 수상 awarded, 공모전 contest, 조교 assistant, 홍보 promotion, 자원봉사 volunteer

(2) Soomi also wrote a cover letter to summarize her resume.

안녕하십니까?

이번에 아람 출판사의 웹 디자이너로 지원하는 윤수미입니다.

저는 한국대학교 디자인학과에서 실용미술학을 전공하고 올해 2월에 졸업할 예정입니다.

대학교 3학년 때 프랑스에 있는 파리 디자인 대학교에서 1년 동안 교환학생을 했고, 그 후 여름에는 디자인 하우스 회사에서 인턴으로 일했습니다. 최근에는 대한민국 디자인 공모전에서 예쁘고 편한 생활 디자인으로 대상을 받았습니다.

저는 어려서부터 책을 좋아하고 책 디자인에 관심이 많아서 졸업 후에는 출판사에서 꼭 일해 보고 싶습니다. 특히 아람 출판사는 좋은 책을 만드는 곳으로 유명하기 때문에 그 책들 한 권 한 권에 독특하고 멋진 디자인을 더해 보고 싶습니다.

감사합니다.

윤수미 올림

최근 recent, 대상 grand prize, 편하다 to be convenient, 생활 life, 어려서부터 from childhood,
관심 interest, 유명하다 to be famous for, 독특하다 to be unique, 멋지다 to be cool, 더하다 to add

Pre-Writing Exercises

1. You went to the Seoul National Park and stopped by a scooter rental shop. Fill out a form to rent an electric scooter for two hours.

이름: _____

나이: _____ 세

휴대폰 번호: _____ – _____ – _____

주민등록번호: _____ – _____

신용카드 번호: _____ – _____

(어린이의 경우 보호자의 번호를 쓰세요.)

날짜: _____ 년 _____ 월 _____ 일

시간: 오전/오후 _____ 시 ~ 오전/오후 _____ 시

종류: ☐ 전동 스쿠터　　☐ 일반 스쿠터

크기: ☐ 남자 어른용　　☐ 여자 어른용　　☐ 어린이용 (12세 이상)

개수: 1　　2　　3　　4　　5

액세서리: ☐ 헬멧　　☐ 장갑　　☐ 바구니　　☐ 물통

위의 내용은 모두 사실입니다. (　　)

사용 중 안전 규칙을 지키겠습니다. (　　)

날짜: _____ 년 _____ 월 _____ 일

서명: _____

세 years old, 주민등록 resident registration, 신용카드 credit card, 어린이 child, 경우 case, 보호자 guardian, 종류 kind, 전동 electric, 일반 general, 크기 size, 어른용 adult use, 이상 more than, 개수 number, 바구니 basket, 내용 content, 사실 truth, 안전 safety, 규칙 rule, 및 and, 서명 signature

2. You are joining the *My Choice Shopping Mall* and filling out its membership form. Complete the e-form below with appropriate information.

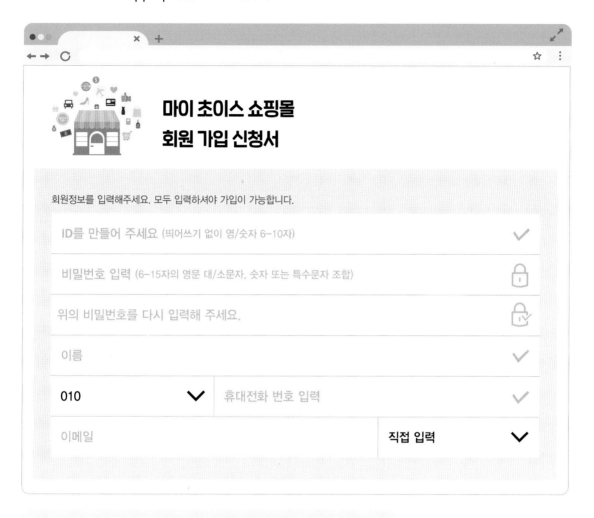

입력 input, 가능하다 to be possible, 띄어쓰기 spacing, 특수 문자 special character, 조합 combination, 직접 direct, 확인 confirm

Interpersonal Writing

1. Next year, you want to study in England and received an email from your department announcing the Study Abroad Scholarship. While applying for the scholarship, you have some questions. Send an email to a person in charge and ask for the following information.

○ Is any country/school/major ok?

○ Is living in an apartment, not a dormitory, ok?

○ Where can I get the application form? Is there an online form?

'빛으로' 유학 장학금 안내

자격: 대학교 1-4학년

사용 방법: 재학 중 해외 유학 (예: 교환 학생, 단기 유학, 어학 연수)

신청 기간: 2월 1일 ~ 3월 30일

금액: 비행기, 학비, 기숙사비

서류: 지원서, 자기소개서, 추천서 2

*연락처: 과 사무실 김유진 yujin@bituro.co.kr

장학금 scholarship, 안내 guide, 자격 qualification, 방법 method, 재학 in school, 해외 유학 study abroad, 단기 short term, 어학 연수 language study, 기간 period, 금액 amount, 과/학과 department

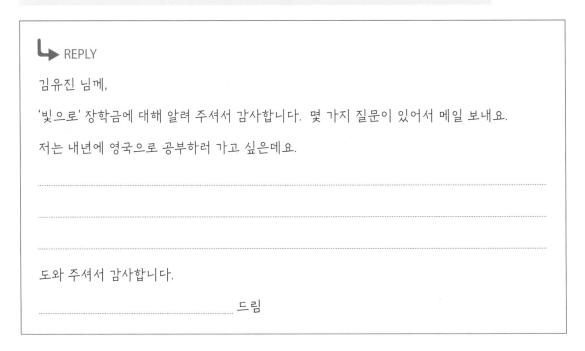

REPLY

김유진 님께,

'빛으로' 장학금에 대해 알려 주셔서 감사합니다. 몇 가지 질문이 있어서 메일 보내요.

저는 내년에 영국으로 공부하러 가고 싶은데요.

....

....

....

도와 주셔서 감사합니다.

.... 드림

2. You decided to buy a membership for a school gym. Send a text message to your friend Jimmy, who has already joined it, to ask several questions.

> You
>
> 지미 씨, 잘 지내요?

Jimmy
> 네, 오랜만이에요. 잘 지내죠?

> You

> 학교 짐에 가입하고 싶은데요.

Jimmy
> 오, 좋은 생각이에요.

> You

Jimmy
> 한 달에 20불이에요.

> You

Jimmy
> 네, 있어요. 거기에 옷하고 운동화를 넣을 수 있어요.

> You

Jimmy
> 한 학기에 25불이에요. 그런데 사물함이 많지 않아서 빨리 사야 돼요.

> You

Jimmy
> 네, 아주 많아요. 무슨 운동을 하고 싶은데요?

> You

Jimmy
> 좋아요. 다 할 수 있어요. 우리 학교 짐은 시설이 참 좋아요.

> You

Jimmy
> 새 학기 첫 번째 주에 사면 5불 더 싸요.

> You

> 고마워요. 지금 살게요. 다음 주말에 같이 운동해요!

Jimmy
> 좋아요. 다음 주 토요일 2시에 만나요!

사물함 locker, 시설 facility

Presentational Writing

1. (1) As a senior at college, you are doing a job search and found a company that you want to join. Instead of a typical resume, the company asks you to submit a free format application. Make your own creative resume including (but not limited to) your basic information and background.

(2) As a supplementary to #1 application, write a personal statement to show your interest and passion to join the company. You can use expressions such as -에 관심이 있다/많다, -고 싶다, -(으)면 좋겠다, -(으)려고 하다 etc.

Writing Tips

신청서/지원서 쓰기 #2
Writing Application Forms #2

In addition to the basics such as **성명, 성별, 생년월일, 주소, 전화번호,** you may need to provide the following information for specific applications. Also, it is not uncommon in Korea that some forms (e.g. resume) require to attach the applicant's photo.

- 학력 academic background
- 경력 work experience
- 수상 award
- 자격(증)/면허(증) license, certificate
- 병역 (군필/미필/면제) military service (fulfilled/unfulfilled/exempted)
- 가족 사항 family information
- 지원 동기 motive

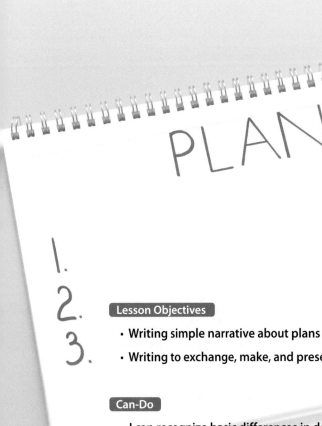

Lesson Objectives

- Writing simple narrative about plans
- Writing to exchange, make, and present about simple personal plans

Can-Do

- I can recognize basic differences in degree of certainty about one's plans.
- I can exchange information about simple plans (e.g. weekends, vacations) with others via text messages, emails, or online using vocabulary and expressions in simple sentences.
- I can state and present my future plans using (strings of) simple sentences and basic connectives.

 Useful Vocabulary, Grammar, and Expressions

1. Vocabulary

(1) ☐ 계획하다 to plan ☐ 계획을 만들다/짜다/세우다 to make plans ☐ 계획이 있다 to have a plan

(2) ☐ 확실히 definitely, for sure ☐ 꼭 without fail ☐ 아마 maybe, probably
☐ 확실하지 않지만 not sure but ☐ 잘 모르(겠)지만 don't know well but

(3) Ordinal numbers: Korean number + 째

- ☐ 첫째
- ☐ 둘째
- ☐ 셋째
- ☐ 넷째
- ☐ 다섯째
- ☐ 여섯째
- ☐ 일곱째
- ☐ 여덟째
- ☐ 아홉째
- ☐ 열째

2. Grammar

① -겠다 I will do

② -(으)ㄹ 거예요 I'm going to

③ -기로 했다 I planned/decided to do

④ -(으)려고 하다 I intend to

⑤ -(으)ㄹ까 (생각)하다 I'm thinking of doing

⑥ -(으)ㄹ 계획이다 I'm planning about doing

⑦ -기 위해 in order to

⑧ -(으)ㄹ래요? Do you wanna? / Shall we?

3. Expressions

① 푹 쉬세요. Have a good rest. / 푹 잘 거예요. I will sleep tight.

② 무슨/어떤 계획이 있으세요? Do you have any plans? / What kind of plans do you have?

③ 계획대로 하는 편이에요. I tend to/usually do as planned.

④ 계획을 실천하겠습니다. I will carry out the plan.

Writing Samples

1. Isabell Joh is a candidate for the vice chair position of the Korea Institute in your regional district. The Institute just posted Isabell's campaign poster on its social media site. Here are Isbell's Action Plans.

안녕하십니까?
저는 이사벨 조입니다.

제가 부회장이 되면
첫째, 일 년에 네 번 (봄, 여름, 가을, 겨울) 문화 행사를 하겠습니다.
둘째, 한 달에 한 번 한국 영화 감상과 토론 모임을 준비하겠습니다.
셋째, 문화 체험 프로그램(예를 들면, 요리, 게임, 서예)을 만들겠습니다.

1번 이사벨 조

부회장 vice president, N이/가 되다 to become N, 서예 calligraphy, 문화 culture, 체험 hands-on experience, 영화 감상 movie screening, 토론 discussion

2. One of the famous lines of the father in the Korean film, 'Parasite' (Director Joon-ho Bong, 2019), is "아들아, 너는 계획이 있구나! (My son, you've got a plan!)." In the end, the son writes a letter to his father to tell him about his plans. Here is part of the son's letter.

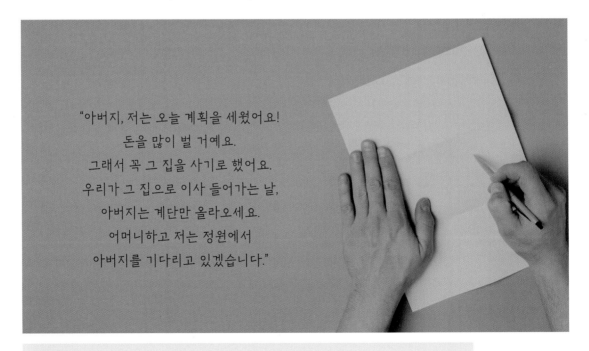

"아버지, 저는 오늘 계획을 세웠어요!
돈을 많이 벌 거예요.
그래서 꼭 그 집을 사기로 했어요.
우리가 그 집으로 이사 들어가는 날,
아버지는 계단만 올라오세요.
어머니하고 저는 정원에서
아버지를 기다리고 있겠습니다."

돈을 벌다 to make money, 이사 들어가다 to move into, 계단 stairs, 올라오다 to come up, 정원 yard

Pre-Writing Exercises

1. Your Korean Cultural Club is polling about its upcoming event for the Lunar New Year. Read the question and response choices carefully and choose one that describes the best for your plan.

❶ 질문: 대면 설날 파티에 참석하겠습니까?

☐ 꼭 참석하겠다

☐ 참석하려고 한다

☐ 참석할까 한다

☐ 잘 모르겠다

☐ 아마 참석할 수 있을 것 같다

☐ 참석 안 하겠다

❷ 질문: 온라인 설날 파티에 참석하겠습니까?

☐ 꼭 참석하겠다

☐ 참석하려고 한다

☐ 참석할까 한다

☐ 잘 모르겠다

☐ 아마 참석할 수 있을 것 같다

☐ 참석 안 하겠다

감사합니다.

대면 in-person/face-to-face, 온라인 online

2. Your school has a special program for students' wellness. One day per month is designated as a well-being day, and all students get a day off. Plan your well-being day for this month so you can recharge yourself and feel refreshed.

My Well-being Day Plan

- Would you stay home, go out, or visit somewhere?
- What would you eat?
- What activities would you do?
- What would you wear?
- Would you enjoy your day alone or invite others?

Get as detailed as you possibly can and follow the guided process.

❶ Make a list (using words, phrases, and simple sentences)

- ○
- ○
- ○
- ○
- ○
- ○

❷ Sort by the certainty of your plan (by using various expressions of certainty)

❸ Write your day plan in sentences.

Interpersonal Writing

1. It is Friday, and Nick, one of your close friends, has sent a message to the group chat to plan a gathering this weekend. Participate in the group chat by responding, asking questions, and reacting to their messages.

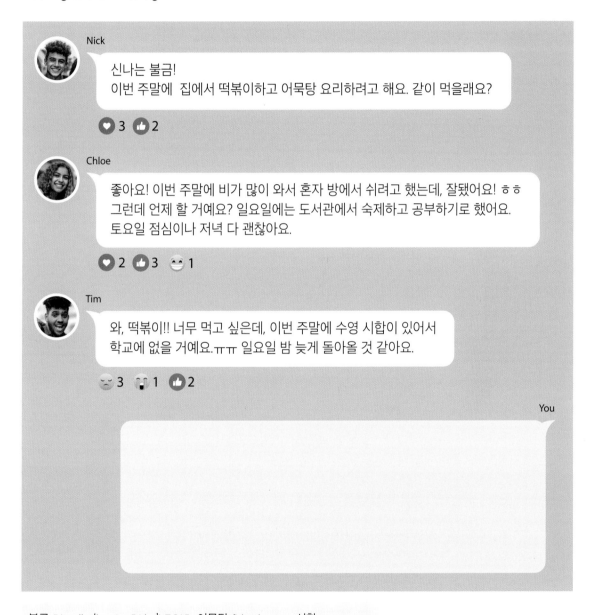

Nick

신나는 불금!
이번 주말에 집에서 떡볶이하고 어묵탕 요리하려고 해요. 같이 먹을래요?

♥ 3 👍 2

Chloe

좋아요! 이번 주말에 비가 많이 와서 혼자 방에서 쉬려고 했는데, 잘됐어요! ㅎㅎ
그런데 언제 할 거예요? 일요일에는 도서관에서 숙제하고 공부하기로 했어요.
토요일 점심이나 저녁 다 괜찮아요.

♥ 2 👍 3 😄 1

Tim

와, 떡볶이!! 너무 먹고 싶은데, 이번 주말에 수영 시합이 있어서
학교에 없을 거예요.ㅠㅠ 일요일 밤 늦게 돌아올 것 같아요.

😠 3 😭 1 👍 2

You

불금 (Literally, 'burning Friday') T.G.I.F., 어묵탕 fish cake soup, 시합 tournament

2. You are a study abroad student at a university in Korea. The Office of Career in the university is administering students' Future Plans Survey. Participate in the survey by providing your responses to the questions.

질문 5. 졸업 후 계획

❶ 졸업 후에 무슨 일을 할 계획입니까?

> 응답
>
>
>
>
>

❷ 그 일을 준비하기 위해 어떤 계획들이 있습니까?

> 응답
>
>
>
>
>

설문에 응답해 주셔서 감사합니다.

응답 response, 준비하다 to prepare, 설문 survey

Presentational Writing

1. You are running for the president position of your club/student council/organization. The election process requires you to submit a poster containing your action plans for running the organization if elected president.

   Present your poster, including the list of your feasible action plans/election promises, with examples in sentences.

2. You are making plans for the upcoming summer break and applying to a short-term Korean language and culture learning program in Korea. The program offers a 4-week session with funding covering tuition, room and board, moderate stipends, and roundtrip airline tickets. The online application form includes a brief description of your plans while in Korea. Propose your plans providing a to-do list (3-5) with short descriptions in sentences.

계획

Writing Tips

-(스)ㅂ니다
Formal Style Sentence Ending

When writing personal statements (such as self-introduction, future plans, etc.) for proposals or applications, the formal style of sentence ending -ㅂ/습니다 is appropriate and commonly used.

헷갈리는 서수
Confusing Ordinal Number

1. 첫 번째 vs. 첫째 first

첫 번째, 두 번째, 세 번째,... and 첫째, 둘째, 셋째,... are interchangable in general. However, 첫째, 둘째, 셋째... are used when describing family members.

> **ex** 첫 번째 사진 the first photo
> 첫째 딸/아들/이모/삼촌 first daughter/son/aunt/uncle

2. 셋째? vs. 세째? third

첫째, 둘째, 셋째, 넷째,... 열한째, 열두째, 열셋째, 열넷째... are correct spellings according to the current standard Korean language regulation. Please note that 둘째 becomes 두째 over ten-digit numbers.

4.1. 장소 후기 Reviewing Places

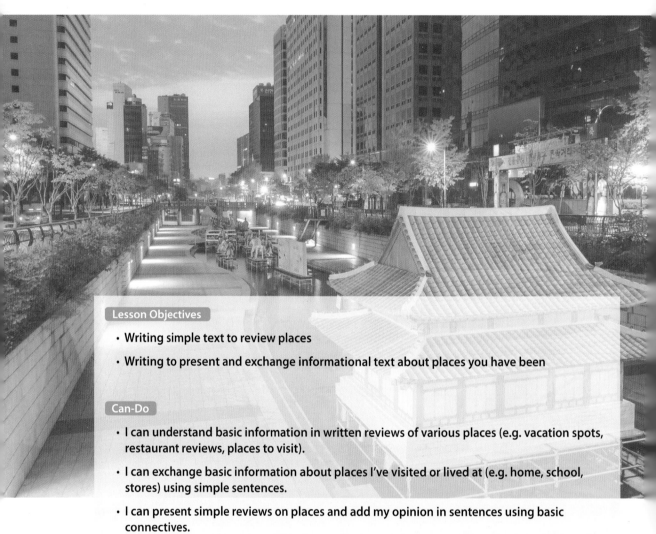

Lesson Objectives

- Writing simple text to review places
- Writing to present and exchange informational text about places you have been

Can-Do

- I can understand basic information in written reviews of various places (e.g. vacation spots, restaurant reviews, places to visit).
- I can exchange basic information about places I've visited or lived at (e.g. home, school, stores) using simple sentences.
- I can present simple reviews on places and add my opinion in sentences using basic connectives.

 Useful Vocabulary, Grammar, and Expressions

1. Vocabulary

(1) ☐ 학교 school ☐ 교실 classroom ☐ 방 room

☐ 기숙사 dormitory ☐ 아파트 apartment ☐ 도서관 library

☐ 식당 restaurant ☐ 맛집 gourmet restaurant ☐ 카페 cafe

☐ 빵집/제과점 bakery ☐ 책방/서점 bookstore ☐ 백화점 department store

☐ 슈퍼 supermarket	☐ 시장 market	☐ 가게 store
☐ 편의점 convenient store	☐ 꽃집 flower shop	☐ 약국 drug store
☐ 극장/영화관 theater	☐ 공원 park	☐ 교회 church
☐ 공항 airport	☐ 집 home/house	☐ 동네 neighborhood
☐ 고향 hometown	☐ 도시 city	☐ 시내 downtown
☐ 시외 suburb		

(2)
☐ 좋다 to be good	☐ 나쁘다 to be bad	☐ 추천하다 to recommend
☐ 넓다 to be spacious	☐ 좁다 to be narrow	☐ 크다 to be big
☐ 작다 to be small	☐ 많다 to be many	☐ 적다 to be little
☐ 조용하다 to be quiet	☐ 시끄럽다 to be noisy	☐ 맛있다 to be delicious
☐ 맛없다 to not be delicious	☐ 친절하다 to be kind	☐ 예쁘다 to be pretty
☐ 아름답다 to be beautiful	☐ 멋있다 to be cool/stylish	☐ 가깝다 to be close
☐ 멀다 to be far	☐ 깨끗하다 to be clean	☐ 더럽다 to be dirty
☐ 싸다 to be cheap	☐ 비싸다 to be expensive	☐ 괜찮다 to be alright
☐ 유명하다 to be famous/popular		

2. Grammar

① -아/아 보다 to try to

② -아/어 본 적이 있다/없다 to have/not have experienced to

3. Expressions

① 가 봤어요? Have you ever been there?

② 어때요/어땠어요? How is/was it?

③ 별로였어요. It was not that good.

④ 꼭 한번 가 보세요. Please be sure to visit.

Writing Samples

1. Sandy plans to visit a local seashore with friends and needs to search for a place to eat. She found a list of reviews for local restaurants and here is one of her choices.

바다의 맛

주소: 강릉시 주문진읍 미도리 37
전화: 033-692-9709
영업 시간: 오전 10시 - 오후 9시

❶ ★★★★★
myseafood 37 해산물이 맛있어요.

❷ ★★★★★
와우와우2 신선해요. 꼭 가 보세요!!!

❸ ★★★★☆
abcdef 바다 바로 옆에 있어서 분위기 좋음. 사람이 많아서 시간이 걸림

❹ ★★★★☆
바다사랑 맛있는데 비싼 편

❺ ★★★☆☆
미미2022 서비스가 별로... 뷰는 멋짐

❻ ★★★★☆
맛집러 오징어 파스타 강추!!! 디저트도 짱!!!

❼ ★★★★★
강릉에_오세요 근처에서 제일 맛있는 식당이에요. 데이트 할 때 추천해요.

> 영업 business, 해산물 seafood, 별 star, 신선하다 to be fresh, 분위기 atmosphere,
> 강추 strongly recommended *(slang)*, 짱 the best *(slang)*

2. Woojoo is an RA (resident assistant) of the Hana Hall in Daehan University. He made a flyer to introduce the dormitory for newly admitted and transferred students this year.

하나 홀에서 하나가 됩시다!!!

우리 하나 기숙사는 ~

- 여학생들은 짝수 층, 남학생들은 홀수 층에 살아요.
- 가장 최근에 만든 기숙사라서 깨끗하고 시설이 좋아요.
- 메인 캠퍼스에서 가까워요. (특히 공대 건물에 가까우니까 공대 학생들에게 추천)
- 식당 음식이 다양하고 맛있어요. (한식/중식/일식/양식 등)
- 1인 1실, 2인 1실, 그리고 4인 1실이 있어요.
- 큰 라운지가 있어요. (소파, 탁구/당구/게임 가능)
- 같이 쓰는 부엌이 있어서 음식을 만들 수 있어요.
- 24시간 여는 컴퓨터실이 있어요.
- 여러 가지 운동 시설이 있어요.
- 매주 재미있는 이벤트가 있어요.
- 선후배 버디 프로그램이 있어서 신입생과 편입생에게 좋습니다.

> 짝수 even number, 홀수 odd number, 시설 facility, 공대 engineering, -(으)니까 because, 다양하다 to be various,
> 탁구 table tennis, 당구 billiard, 선후배 senior-junior, 신입생 freshman, 편입생 transfer student

Pre-Writing Exercises

1. You are a volunteer of the **Get-To-Know School Library Project** at your college. Fill out the survey by reviewing the libraries on campus. Your opinion is important as the project committee will improve the facilities based on the survey results.

> Please review each library.
>
> 1. 도서관 A: 중앙 도서관
>
>   중앙 도서관은 크고 넓어요. 사람이 많아서 시끄러워요. 그리고 물이나 음료수를 마실 수 없어서 조금 불편해요. 저는 보통 책을 빌리러 중앙 도서관에 가요.
>
> 2. 도서관 B:
>
>   ....
>
>   ....
>
> 3. 도서관 C:
>
>   ....
>
>   ....

중앙 central

2. You are taking an elementary Korean course this semester at college. For an individual project, you will share **My favorite vacation place** with your classmates who come from various countries. Choose two places that you've traveled and provide your review of each place with pros and cons.

여행지 #1	여행지 #2 ....
좋은 점	좋은 점
○	○ ....
○	○ ....
○	○ ....
나쁜 점	나쁜 점
○	○ ....
○	○ ....
○	○ ....

여행지/ 여행 장소 Travel spot/destination

Interpersonal Writing

1. You are working for the Campus Housing Department at Hankook University. Please respond to each email inquiry from incoming freshmen asking about dormitories on campus.

(1) 보낸 사람: 데이빗 황

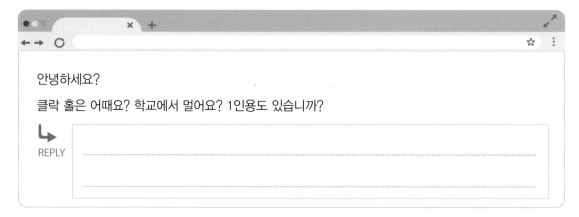

안녕하세요?

클락 홀은 어때요? 학교에서 멀어요? 1인용도 있습니까?

REPLY

(2) 보낸 사람: 스테파니 엘리엇

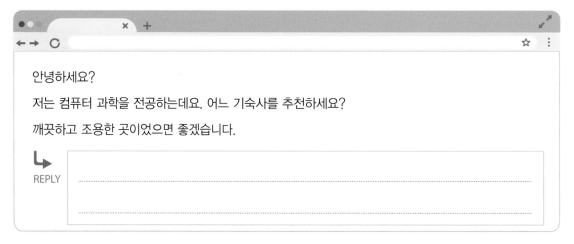

안녕하세요?

저는 컴퓨터 과학을 전공하는데요. 어느 기숙사를 추천하세요?

깨끗하고 조용한 곳이었으면 좋겠습니다.

REPLY

(3) 보낸 사람: 린다 첸

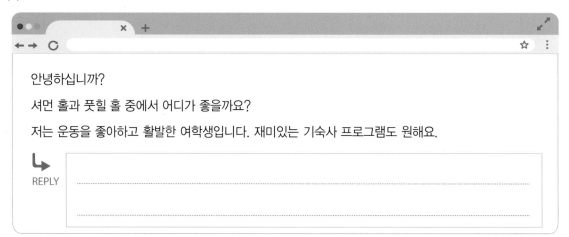

안녕하십니까?

셔먼 홀과 풋힐 홀 중에서 어디가 좋을까요?

저는 운동을 좋아하고 활발한 여학생입니다. 재미있는 기숙사 프로그램도 원해요.

REPLY

2. You were born and raised in Hawaii. You went to college in New York, then you are living in San Francisco now. Today, you received a letter from your hometown junior Yoori in Korea who plans to apply for an exchange student program and asks for your opinion about these places. Reply to her by reviewing each place you have lived in.

안녕하세요? 잘 지내시죠?

저도 잘 있어요. 대학 생활은 좀 바쁘지만 재미있어요.

저는 내년에 미국에 교환학생으로 가려고 해요. 뉴욕, 샌프란시스코, 그리고 하와이에 있는 대학 중 한 군데 가고 싶은데...

아직 못 정했어요. 선배는 세 곳에 모두 살아 봤으니까 저한테 추천해 주실 수 있어요? 어디가 좋을까요?

고마워요. 내년에 미국에서 봐요!!!

한국에서 유리가

REPLY

1. You are a member of the Student Council at Mirae University. This semester, the organization is making a booklet of *20 Must-Visit Places While Attending Mirae University*. List the hot spots to introduce your favorite places near campus to recommend them to other students.

(1) Food (restaurant, cafe, bakery, supermarket, etc.)

(2) Shopping (shop, department store, etc.)

(3) Convenient facilities (hair salon, gym, theater, etc.)

(4) Dating places

Writing Tips

 후기에 쓰이는 신조어/줄임말/은어

Newly-coined words/Shortened words/Slang used in Online Reviews

Recently, newly coined words are widely used on internet communities. They may not be "official" words that are listed in the dictionary, but it can be helpful to know (and use) them for understanding casual written texts. Here are some examples that are commonly used in reviews.

ex 대박 It's dope.
  강추 strongly recommend
  비추 not recommend
  짱 the best thing
  뷰 맛집 restaurant with a great view
  인스타 맛집 restaurant which is good for pictures for instagram
  맛잘알 (맛을 잘 아는 사람) person who knows taste
  내돈내산 (내 돈 주고 내가 산 물건) things that I bought with my own money

Short acronyms are also commonly used for some popular places.

ex 스벅 Starbucks, 파바 Paris Baguette, 맥날 McDonald's, 피방 PC room, 고터 Express Bus Terminal Shops

4.2. 쇼핑 후기 Shopping Places

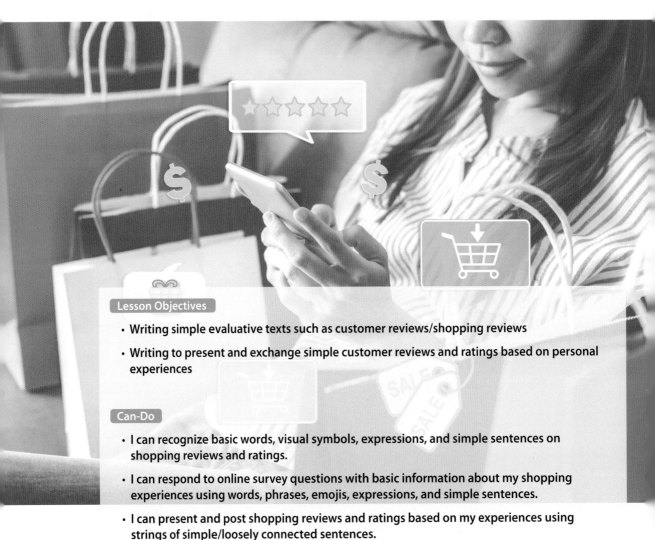

Lesson Objectives

- Writing simple evaluative texts such as customer reviews/shopping reviews
- Writing to present and exchange simple customer reviews and ratings based on personal experiences

Can-Do

- I can recognize basic words, visual symbols, expressions, and simple sentences on shopping reviews and ratings.
- I can respond to online survey questions with basic information about my shopping experiences using words, phrases, emojis, expressions, and simple sentences.
- I can present and post shopping reviews and ratings based on my experiences using strings of simple/loosely connected sentences.

Useful Vocabulary, Grammar, and Expressions

1. Vocabulary

(1) 가격/값 price
서비스 (customer) service
판매 selling
거래 deal/dealings/transactions (business)

배송료 shipping fee
구입 purchase
후기 review

앱 app
구매 buying
세일/할인 sale (discount)
환불 refund

☐ 교환 exchange   ☐ 반품 return   ☐ 현금 cash

☐ 카드 (credit) card   ☐ 추천 recommended   ☐ 비추천 not recommended

☐ 만족 satisfactory   ☐ 불만족 unsatisfactory   ☐ 매우 very

☐ 되게 very

(2)   ☐ 싸다 to be cheap   ☐ 비싸다 to be expensive   ☐ 편리하다 to be convenient

☐ 불편하다 to be uncomfortable/ inconvenient   ☐ 실망하다 to be disappointed

2. Grammar

① -(으)ㄴ 편이다 kind of, rather

② 별로 안 not really, not particularly

③ -지 마세요 Don't

④ -아/어 보다 try doing something

⑤ -게 -ly

⑥ -(으)ㄴ 가요/나요? I am wondering if *(a little softer than -아/어요?)*

3. Expressions

① 잘/잘못 샀어요. It was a good/wrong buy.

② 싸게/비싸게 샀어요. I got it for a cheap/expensive price.

③ 바가지 썼어요. I got ripped off.

④ 마음에 (쏙) 들어요. I love it (a lot).

⑤ 질이 좋아요/나빠요. Its quality is good/bad.

⑥ 믿을 수 있어요/없어요. It is reliable/unreliable.

⑦ 믿을 만해요. It is worth relying on.

Writing Samples

1. Megan recently purchased a sweater from an online shopping mall and left her review on its customer review section.

강추!!

일주일 전에 이 스웨터를 샀어요. 20% 세일을 해서 싸게 샀어요. 색깔과 사이즈도 저한테 잘 맞아요. 또 이 스웨터는 아주 편해요. 집에서 빨 수도 있어요.

정말 잘 산 것 같아요. 마음에 쏙 들어요!

아, 그런데 배송료가 좀 비싸요. 그리고 환불하고 교환이 안 돼요. 그래서 4점을 줬어요.^^

강추('강력 추천') two thumbs up; it is strongly recommended, 맞다 to fit, 편하다 to be comfortable, 빨다 to wash (laundry), 점 points

2. Austin purchased an acoustic guitar from "중고 시장," a mobile second-hand market platform. Refer to his review of this vendor for future purchases in your local community on this platform.

기타월드 님과 거래가 어땠나요?

 별로예요   좋아요!   최고예요!

- 제가 있는 곳까지 와서 거래했어요.
- 친절하고 믿을 수 있어요.
- 시간 약속을 잘 지켜요.
- 응답이 빨라요.

중고 second-hand/used, 시장 market, 통기타 acoustic guitar, 월드 world, 최고 the best, 거래 dealing; transaction, 믿을 수 있다 to be reliable; trustworthy, 응답 response, 별로 so-so/mediocre

1. (1) What have you recently purchased? Choose three items you've bought and rate them.

#1. ....(item)
    ☐ 만족   ☐ 실망

#2. ....
    ☐ 최고예요   ☐ 좋아요   ☐ 별로예요   ☐ 안 좋아요.

#3. ....
    ☐ 추천   ☐ 비추천

(2) Now, the online shopping vendor asks you to provide your review on each item on the platform. Write in sentences using suggested keywords and expressions.

#1. ....
☐ ....
    ....
    ....
    ....

#2. ....
☐ ....
    ....
    ....
    ....

#3. ....
☐ ....
    ....
    ....
    ....

> 판매자, 가격, 질, 서비스, 배송(료), 환불, 교환, 거래, 득템, 최고, 강추, 별로,
> 싸다, 비싸다, 만족하다, 실망하다, 잘 사다, 마음에 들다, 믿을 수 있다

득템 good deal/ good–buy ('good item'–좋은 아이템)

2. You are searching for a bicycle from your local flea market platform on the internet. You found this post and have an interest in the bicycle. Send the seller a chat message. Make sure to include several questions.

쌩쌩 자전거

150,000원

쌩쌩 자전거 팝니다. 2년 전에 샀는데, 많이 안 타서 새 자전거 같아요.

헬멧도 있어요. 원하면 공짜로 드릴게요. 질문 있으면 채팅으로 연락 주세요.

You

헬멧 helmet, 채팅 chat

Interpersonal Writing

1. You bought a coffee table for your new off-campus apartment from a local second-hand market on social media. Your next-door neighbor is also interested in purchasing a chair from the same seller and asks you about your shopping experience with the seller. Respond to the following text messages.

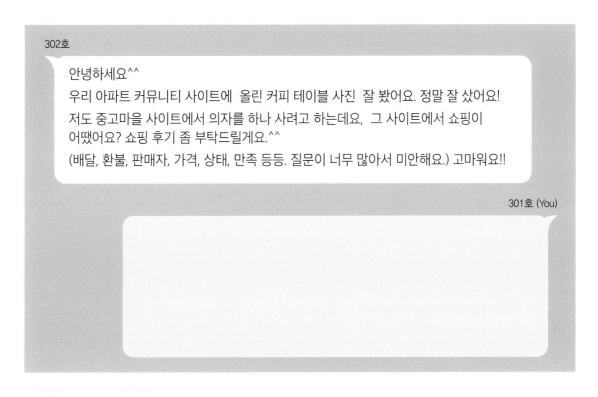

302호

안녕하세요^^
우리 아파트 커뮤니티 사이트에 올린 커피 테이블 사진 잘 봤어요. 정말 잘 샀어요!
저도 중고마을 사이트에서 의자를 하나 사려고 하는데요, 그 사이트에서 쇼핑이
어땠어요? 쇼핑 후기 좀 부탁드릴게요.^^
(배달, 환불, 판매자, 가격, 상태, 만족 등등. 질문이 너무 많아서 미안해요.) 고마워요!!

301호 (You)

등(등) etc., 301호 APT #301

2. The customer service department of the internet shopping mall company sent you a customer review survey about your recent purchase. Provide your response.

안녕하십니까?
다사가 쇼핑몰을 이용해 주셔서 감사합니다.
아래 설문에 응답해 주시면 감사하겠습니다.

(1) 구입하신 물건에 만족하십니까?

☐ 예   ☐ 아니요

이유: _____

(2) 배송 서비스는 어땠습니까?

☐ 좋음   ☐ 보통   ☐ 나쁨

이유: _____

(3) 다사가 쇼핑몰을 자주 이용하십니까?

☐ 예   ☐ 아니요

이유: _____

(4) 다사가 쇼핑몰을 추천하시겠습니까?

☐ 강추   ☐ 추천   ☐ 비추천

이유: _____

(5) 다사가 쇼핑몰 이용에 불편하신 점이나 바라는 점이 있으면 알려 주시기 바랍니다.

다시 한번 다사가 쇼핑몰을 이용해 주셔서 감사합니다.
할인권 잊지 마세요.

할인권 discount coupon

Presentational Writing

1. Do you have any preference between online shopping and in-store shopping? Do you have any purchased items that you were disappointed in? What was one thing you bought for a good deal? Choose one item you highly recommend or don't recommend, and share your experience.

These are just suggested outline points to include but not limited to:

- Overall final rate
- Do you recommend it? Why or why not?
- How about price, quality, and service?
- Are you satisfied with your purchased item? Why or why not?
- How was the transaction process?
- How about the seller you directly purchased from?
- Any additional comments?

Writing Tips

Yes/No 대답하기

Properly Responding Yes/No

1. 네 vs 예 (Yes)

   Both mean 'Yes' and are interchangeable as synonyms.

2. 아니오 vs 아니요 (No)

   The correct spelling of 'No,' as in Yes/No, is 아니요 in Korean. Its casual form is 아니, and polite form is 아니요.

제품 사용 후기 쓰기

Product Review Writing

Here are some simple steps to help you write a good product review.

1. Be Honest: Say what you like and don't like about the product.

2. Describe the Product: Tell what the product looks like and what it does.

3. Share Your Experience: Talk about how you used the product and what happened.

4. Think of Your Readers: Write in a way that is easy for your readers to understand.

5. Recommend or Not: At the end, say if you think people should buy the product or not.

Also, utilize the useful expressions presented in this lesson to make your review informative and engaging.

비교문 쓰기

Writing a Comparison

When you write about similarities and differences, it is useful to incorporate the following expressions:

1. N보다 더/덜 more/less than

> ex 생각한 것보다 더 좋았습니다.

2. -(으)ㄴ/는 반면에 whereas

> ex 종류가 다양하지 않은 반면에 디자인과 상태는 마음에 쏙 들어요.

3. -에 비해서 comparing to

> ex 다른 가게에 비해서 가격이 쌉니다

4. N 만큼 as~ as

> ex 중고 제품도 새 제품만큼 좋습니다.

4.3. | 활동 후기 Reviewing Activities

Lesson Objectives

- Writing simple text to review activities
- Writing to describe and share informational text about activities you have done

Can-Do

- I can identify basic information in various activity reviews (e.g. volunteer service activity, internship, part-time work).
- I can exchange basic information in spontaneous written communication about activities I was involved in (e.g. school activities, jobs) using practiced or memorized words, phrases, and simple sentences.
- I can present reviews on activities and add my opinion in simple sentences and loosely connected sentences.

 Useful Vocabulary, Grammar, and Expressions

1. Vocabulary

(1)   ☐ 활동 activity   ☐ 과외 활동 extracurricular activity   ☐ 경험 experience

      ☐ 동아리/동호회 club   ☐ 자원 봉사 volunteer   ☐ 가정 교사 tutor (at home)

      ☐ 과외 private tutoring   ☐ 아르바이트(=알바) part-time job   ☐ 인턴 intern

(2) ☐ 쉽다 to be easy　　　☐ 어렵다 to be difficult　　　☐ 힘들다 to be hard

☐ 재미있다 to be interesting　　　☐ 재미없다 to not be interesting　　　☐ 즐겁다 to be fun

☐ 보람(이) 있다 to be worthwhile　　　☐ 돈(을) 벌다 to earn money

2. Grammar

① -아/아 보다 to try to

② -ㄴ/은 적이 있다/없다, -아/어 본 적이 있다/없다 to have/ not have experience to

③ -(으)ㄴ데/는데 and/but *(giving background information)*

④ -지만 however

3. Expressions

① 어때요/어땠어요? How is/was it?

② 한번 해 보세요. Please give it a try.

③ 해볼 만해요. It's worth a try.

④ 좋은 경험이었어요. It was a good experience.

Writing Samples

1. Bill is a high school senior in the US planning to major in computer science at college. He wants to apply to a college in Korea, as he has been fascinated by Korean language and culture, and hopes to have first-hand experience there. During the application process, he wrote a statement describing his extracurricular activities.

컴퓨터 도우미에서 컴퓨터 전공자로

제 열 살 생일에 아버지께서 생일 선물로 컴퓨터를 사 주셨습니다. 저는 그 선물을 너무 좋아해서 매일 몇 시간씩 컴퓨터를 가지고 놀았고, 곧 컴퓨터를 아주 잘 하게 되었습니다. 중학교 때는 재미있는 게임 프로그램을 여러 개 만들었는데 친구들이 아주 좋아했습니다. 고등학교 때는 매년 해커톤에 참여하고, 프로그래밍 대회에서 상도 많이 받았습니다. 그리고 주말마다 동네에 있는 양로원에서 할아버지, 할머니들께 컴퓨터를 가르쳐 드렸습니다. 학교 수업 때문에 좀 바빴지만 4년 동안 이 자원봉사를 계속했는데 정말 보람이 있었습니다.

저는 대학교에서 컴퓨터 과학을 전공하려고 합니다. 컴퓨터 역사와 이론도 배우고 프로그래밍도 더 알고 싶습니다. 그리고 졸업 후에는 구글이나 페이스북에서 일하고 싶습니다.

도우미 helper, 해커톤 hackathon, 참여하다 to participate, 대회 competition, 계속하다 to continue, 역사 history, 이론 theory, 졸업 graduation, 후 after

2. Jasmine got a job teaching English in Korea for next year. She arrived there six months early so that she could gain some familiarity with Korean culture. Now, she is looking for a part-time job before starting her full-time work. She found some reviews at the Alba Nara (알바나라), an online site for part-time positions.

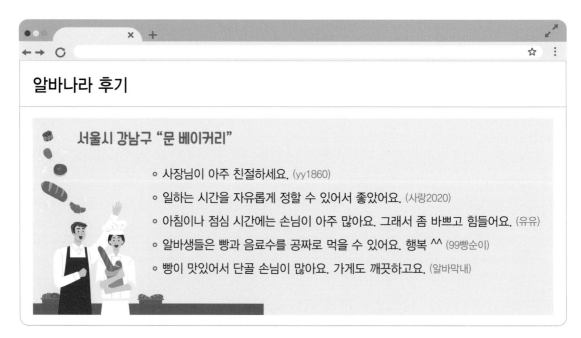

알바나라 후기

서울시 강남구 "문 베이커리"

- 사장님이 아주 친절하세요. (yy1860)
- 일하는 시간을 자유롭게 정할 수 있어서 좋았어요. (사랑2020)
- 아침이나 점심 시간에는 손님이 아주 많아요. 그래서 좀 바쁘고 힘들어요. (유유)
- 알바생들은 빵과 음료수를 공짜로 먹을 수 있어요. 행복 ^^ (99빵순이)
- 빵이 맛있어서 단골 손님이 많아요. 가게도 깨끗하고요. (알바막내)

서울시 종로구 "한국의 집" 식당

- 밤 늦게까지 일해야 돼서 힘들었어요 ㅠㅠ (김유미)
- 매니저가 별로... (kjkkj22)
- 일은 좀 어렵지만 오후 2시부터 4시까지 휴식 시간이 있음. (한식사랑)
- 주급은 적당해요. 그리고 팁도 많이 받아요. (77gks)
- 술 마시고 취한 손님을 대하기 어렵지만 대체로 일하기 편했어요. (알바막내)

서울시 은평구 "뉴월드 피씨방"

- 시설이 좋아서 늘 손님이 많아요. (oldboy20)
- 같이 일하는 동료들이 좋고 주인 아저씨도 친절합니다. (내가최고야)
- 이 피씨방에서 음식 서빙하는데 너무 힘들어요. 그만 일하고 싶어요. (울고싶다!!!)
- 돈을 제대로 안 줬어요. (필승코리아)
- 24시간 문을 열기 때문에 알바 자리가 많아요. (Snow**)

사장님 owner, 자유롭게 freely, 알바생 part-time worker, 공짜로 for free, 행복 happiness, 단골 regular customer, 휴식 rest, 주급 weekly salary, 적당하다 to be appropriate, 취하다 to get drunk, 대체로 generally, 시설 facility, 동료 colleague, 제대로 properly

Pre-Writing Exercises

1. Your classmate Steve set you up on a blind date (소개팅) with his roommate Mark. You met Mark today at a cafe near campus and had a wonderful time. Let's write about your first blind date experience.

(1) First, list things in Korean about Mark.

○ 전공, 학년 ....

○ 가족, 고향 ....

○ 외모 ....

○ 성격 ....

○ 취미 ....

○ 기타 ....

외모 appearance, 성격 personality, 기타 the others

(2) Next, list things in Korean that you and Mark did together today.

○ ....

○ ....

○ ....

○ ....

(3) Using your memo above, write a journal to describe your blind date experience today.

오늘 소개팅을 했어요. 한국어 수업을 같이 듣는 친구 스티브가 룸메이트인 마크를 소개해 줬어요. 우리는 12시에 학교 앞 카페에서 만났어요.

우리는 이번 주말에 다시 만나기로 했어요. 날씨가 좋으면 바닷가에 가려고 해요.

마크가 친절하고 재미있어서 참 좋아요^^ (스티브, 고마워요~)

소개팅 blind date

Interpersonal Writing

1. You worked as a campus tour guide at your college last year. You received an email today from Tara who is interested in working as a guide. Share your experience with her by reviewing the part-time position.

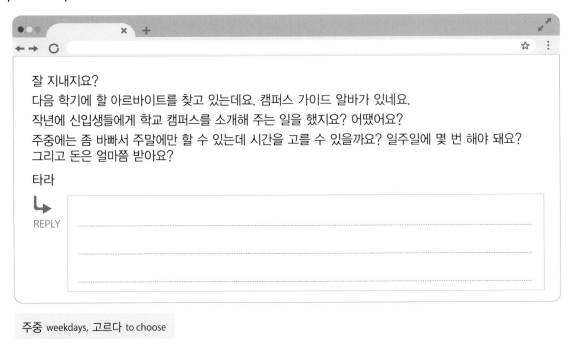

잘 지내지요?

다음 학기에 할 아르바이트를 찾고 있는데요. 캠퍼스 가이드 알바가 있네요.

작년에 신입생들에게 학교 캠퍼스를 소개해 주는 일을 했지요? 어땠어요?

주중에는 좀 바빠서 주말에만 할 수 있는데 시간을 고를 수 있을까요? 일주일에 몇 번 해야 돼요? 그리고 돈은 얼마쯤 받아요?

타라

REPLY

주중 weekdays, 고르다 to choose

2. You applied for the IT Department of Google Korea and got an email from their office of Human Resources (HR) asking more about your experience related to the field. Reply to the inquiry by mentioning your relevant courses, work experience, summer internships, and club activities.

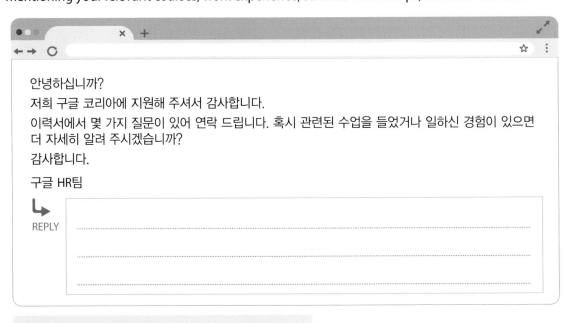

안녕하십니까?

저희 구글 코리아에 지원해 주셔서 감사합니다.

이력서에서 몇 가지 질문이 있어 연락 드립니다. 혹시 관련된 수업을 들었거나 일하신 경험이 있으면 더 자세히 알려 주시겠습니까?

감사합니다.

구글 HR팀

REPLY

지원하다 to apply, 이력서 resume, 관련 relation, 자세히 in detail

Presentational Writing

1. Last year, you participated in TaLK (Teach and Learn in Korea), a government-sponsored English teaching program. During weekdays, you taught kids at elementary schools in rural areas of Korea. During weekends, you learned Korean language and culture. After returning to the US, you've been requested to write a review about the experience by the program organizers. Choose two activities (one as a teacher and the other as a student) that you want to share with future applicants and write reviews.

첫 번째 활동: "저는 선생님으로서 영어를 가르쳤어요!"

두 번째 활동: "저는 학생으로서 한국어와 문화를 배웠어요!"

—(으)로서 as, for

2. As a mentor for new college students, you need to write an article for a school magazine. The topic of this month is "The Bucket List While in College." Choose the most memorable and meaningful activity of your college years and write about it.

대학 졸업하기 전에 꼭 해 봐야 할 활동

Writing Tips

헷갈리는 띄어쓰기

Confusing Spacing

Spacing is an essential part to know in order to write Korean sentences appropriately. It is especially so when use of a space can change the whole meaning you intend to write. For example, "아버지가방에들어가셨어요." can be ambiguous as it can mean "Father entered the room." but also it can mean "(Someone) entered the father's bag."

Please refer to the separate chapter of this book for reviewing general spacing rules. Below are some examples of common mistakes.

1. 안/못 : When 안/못 is used for negation, there is a space between 안/못 and a verb. However, when it is a part of a word, there is no space.

   안 되다 to not become, to not work   `ex` 열심히 공부했지만 시험에 안 됐어요.
   안되다 to feel sorry   `ex` 그 사람은 많이 아파요. 참 안됐어요.

   못 되다 cannot become   `ex` 교수가 되고 싶었는데 못 됐어요.
   못되다 to be mean   `ex` 그 사람은 너무 못됐어요.

   잘 못해요 to not do well   `ex` 저는 수영을 잘 못해요.
   잘못해요 to do wrong   `ex` 제가 잘못했습니다. 죄송합니다.

2. 밖에: When 밖에 is used as an adverb there is a space before it. However, when it is a particle, 밖에 is attached to a noun and no space is necessary.

   밖에 outside   `ex` 지금 밖에 비가 와요.
   N밖에 only   `ex` 커피밖에 안 마셨어요.

3. 번: When 한 번 means 'one time', there is a space between the number and the counter. However, when it means 'just', there is no space in between.

   한 번 once   `ex` 그 식당에서 한 번 먹어 봤어요.
   한번 just   `ex` 그 식당에 한번 가 보세요.

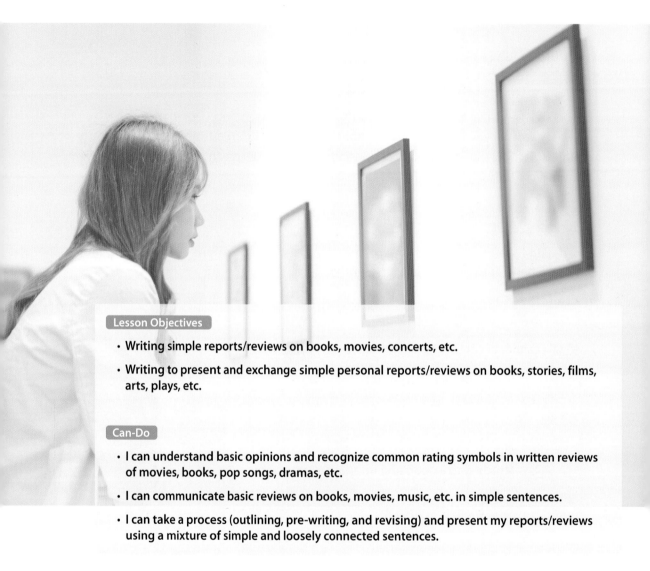

4.4. | 감상 후기 Reports/Reviews

Lesson Objectives

- Writing simple reports/reviews on books, movies, concerts, etc.
- Writing to present and exchange simple personal reports/reviews on books, stories, films, arts, plays, etc.

Can-Do

- I can understand basic opinions and recognize common rating symbols in written reviews of movies, books, pop songs, dramas, etc.
- I can communicate basic reviews on books, movies, music, etc. in simple sentences.
- I can take a process (outlining, pre-writing, and revising) and present my reports/reviews using a mixture of simple and loosely connected sentences.

Useful Vocabulary, Grammar, and Expressions

1. Vocabulary

(1)
    ☐ 감상 appreciation   ☐ 문학 literature   ☐ 영화 movie

    ☐ 이야기 story   ☐ 미술 fine art   ☐ 독서 reading

    ☐ 드라마 drama   ☐ 음악 music   ☐ 케이팝 K-Pop

    ☐ 한류 Korean Wave   ☐ 연극 play   ☐ 무대 stage

음악회/콘서트 concert	공연 performance	극장 theater
미술관 art gallery	전시회 exhibition	가수 singer
가사 lyrics	작가 writer	작곡가 composer
감독 director	배우 actor/actress	연기 acting
시작 beginning	중간 middle	끝/결말 end
내용 content	줄거리 plot/synopsis	명장면 best scene
명대사 best line	강점 strength	약점 weakness
좋은 점 pros	나쁜 점 cons	

(2)

장르 genre	액션 영화 action movie	공포 영화 horror movie
코미디 comedy	로맨틱 코미디 (로코) romantic comedy	
사극 historical drama	공상 과학 science fiction	환타지 fantasy
다큐멘터리 documentary	스포츠 sports	

(3)

전통적 traditional	예술적 artistic	교육적 educational
세계적 world-wide	감동적 heartwarming	전체적 overall

(4)

결국 after all	드디어 finally (yearned)	마침내 finally
끝에 at the end	끝으로 lastly	

(5)

재미있다/재미없다 to be interesting/not interesting		무섭다 to be scary
웃기다 to be funny	슬프다 to be sad	유치하다 to be childish/cheesy
어렵다 to be difficult		

2. Grammar

① -아/어지다 become

② -아/어지는 느낌이다 feeling of

③ -아/어야겠다 I think I should

④ -아/어 보니까 I try something and then discover/learn something

⑤ N을/를 통해서 through

⑥ N에 대해서/대한 about

⑦ -기에 좋다 good for

⑧ -(으)ㄹ수록 더/덜 the more/less

3. Expressions

① 감동 받았어요. I was touched.

② 감동적이에요./ 감동을 줘요. It is touching.

③ 좋은/나쁜 평을 받았어요. It received rave/harsh reviews.

④ 인기가 있어요/없어요/많아요. It is popular/not popular/highly popular.

⑤ 관심을 끌고 있어요. It is attracting attention.

⑥ 기억에 남아요. It is memorable.

⑦ 그저 그래요/그랬어요. It is/was so-so.

Writing Samples

1. Esther is a big fan of the K-Pop idol group 'Z-Power.' Z-Power just released their new music video on the Neotube site. Esther left a comment on the site.

Z-Power 공식 채널   785,046 Views

에스터
새 뮤직 비디오 너~~~~무 멋있어요. 최고예요! 춤, 노래, 가사 모두 환상적이네요!

JM
이 뮤직 비디오는 영화 같아요. 볼 때마다 기분이 정말 좋아져요. 완전 대박!

아미
이 노래를 들을 때마다 행복해요. 세계 최고예요! 감사해요~

환상적 fantastic

2. Kadia is on vacation and trying to binge-watch a K-Drama series. Her friends recommended the Squid Game (오징어 게임), and Kadia is checking some reviews on it in an online community.

오징어 게임 별점/ 한 줄 평

★ ★ ★ ★ ★
정말 재미있게 봤어요. 어렸을 때 자주 하던 놀이들이 거의 다 나왔네요. 강추!

★ ★ ★ ★ ★
보면서 속이 시원해졌어요. 웃고 울고 무섭고 화나고 슬프고… 다 느낄 수 있어요.

★ ★ ★ ★ ★
배우들 연기가 정말 대단해요. 그런데 게임에서 지면 죽어야 돼서 슬프고 무서워요 ㅠ

★ ★ ★ ★ ★
내용은 좀 어둡지만 드라마를 통해 현실적인 문제를 보여주는 것 같아요…

별점 star rating (review points), 한 줄 평 one line review comment, 놀이 playing/game, −던 used to do, 거의 almost, 속이 시원하다 to be refreshing, 대단하다 amazing, 지다 to lose, 현실적 realistic, 문제 problem

Pre-Writing Exercises

1. You are a staff reporter of the online community K-Movie Appreciation Club. You are excited to contribute your report to the club's forum featuring the movie you recently watched.

   As usual, first, you create an outline for your report. Then, write the first draft, filling in each part.

K-영화 감상 동호회

감상 후기

❶ 제목 .... **❷ 장르** ....

❸ 감독 .... **❹ 배우** ....

❺ 별점 ☆ ☆ ☆ ☆ ☆

❻ 한 줄 평 ....

❼ 줄거리

    시작 ....

    ....

    중간 ....

    ....

    끝 ....

    ....

❽ 전체적 느낌/감상 ....

❾ 명장면 ....

❿ 명대사 ....

⓫ 강점 ....

⓬ 약점 ....

⓭ 추천/비추천? 이유

....

....

....

....

Interpersonal Writing

1. You are a member of the online community movie club *Cinema Village*. Your special interest group is K-Movies. You are now in the group chat room to join the conversation. Interact with your groupmates by asking questions and responding to their postings.

시네마 마을
K-Movie SIG

안녕하세요?
제 친구들이 외국인들인데요, 한류에 관심이 아주 많아요. 그래서 한국영화 한 편 추천해 주고 싶은데요,
무슨 영화가 좋을까요?

⤷ 댓글 달기

....

....

....

오, 강추? 그래요? 고마워요! 그런데 그 영화 어떤 영화예요?
슬퍼요? 사랑 얘기? 무서워요? 로코? 유명한 배우들도 나와요? 왜 그 영화 좋아했어요?
(질문이 많아서 미안해요^^)

⤷ 댓글 달기

....

....

....

....

....

....

....

....

댓글 달기 posting a comment, 로코 romantic comedy, 사랑 얘기/이야기 love-story

2. You are in your Korean class discussion forum on the course management platform. The topic of discussion for this week is about a traditional Korean story, **청개구리 *(The Green Frog)*.** Read the story and participate in the discussion by writing your reading responses on each prompt.

옛날에 엄마 청개구리하고 아들 청개구리가 살았어요. 아들 청개구리는 개구쟁이였어요. 그래서 엄마 청개구리의 말을 잘 듣지 않고 항상 반대로 했어요.

엄마 청개구리; "아들, 개굴개굴 해야지."

아들 청개구리: "굴개굴개"

엄마 청개구리: "밥 먹자"

아들 청개구리: "밖에서 놀래요."

엄마 청개구리: "일어나, 학교 가야지."

아들 청개구리: "지금 잘래요."

엄마 청개구리는 아들 청개구리가 말을 잘 듣지 않아서 걱정을 많이 했어요. 어느 날 엄마 청개구리는 많이 아팠어요. 그래서 아들 청개구리에게 말했어요.

엄마 청개구리 "아들아, 엄마가 죽으면 산에 묻지 말고, 냇가에 묻어 줘."

아들 청개구리 " ……"

엄마 청개구리는 돌아가셨어요. 아들 청개구리는 엄마의 말을 잘 듣지 않은 것을 후회했어요. 그래서 엄마 청개구리의 마지막 말대로 하기로 하고 엄마 청개구리를 냇가에 묻었어요.

비가 올 때마다 아들 청개구리는 냇가에서 엄마 무덤이 떠내려갈까 봐 울었어요.

"개굴개굴 개굴개굴"

❶ 이야기를 읽고 어떤 느낌을 받았어요? 왜요?

❷ 이야기를 어린이들에게 추천 하겠어요, 안 하겠어요? 왜요?

❸ 이야기에 별점을 주세요. 왜요?
☆ ☆ ☆ ☆ ☆

❹ 이야기를 읽고 한 줄 평을 써 보세요.

개굴개굴 ribbit-ribbit, 아들 son, 반대로 opposite of, 냇가 stream side, 묻다 to bury, 무덤 grave, 산 mountain, 떠내려가다 washed away, -(으)ㄹ까 봐(서) to be worried/afraid that someone/something would, 개구쟁이 mischievous child, 한 줄 평 one line review, 돌아가시다 to pass away

Presentational Writing

1. You are a member of the library committee in your local community. The committee is selecting a summer reading list for children in K-6. Your assigned task in this process is to write a short report of the story, 청개구리.

   Based on your reading responses in the Interpersonal Writing section, fill out the book report form and submit it to the committee.

희망 도서관 어린이 여름 독서 추천

성명		년 월 일	추천	☐ 네	☐ 아니요
책 제목		별점 ☆ ☆ ☆ ☆ ☆	추천 학년 ☐ 유치원 ☐ 초등학교 _____ 학년		

줄거리

좋은/나쁜 점

추천/비추천 이유

질문 / 의견

제목 title, 여름 summer, 독서 reading (as a hobby), 어린이 children, 유치원 kindergarten, 학년 grade (school year), 초등학교 elementary school, 줄거리 storyline, 의견 opinion, 좋은/나쁜 점 good/bad points

2. The Korean Cultural Center announced a call for submission to their annual publication of 'Riding K-Wave.' You are invited as a special guest contributor to share your report essay.

The Editor-in Chief requested you for the following information:

What is your favorite movie, music, song, drama, story, book, animation, or concert?

Choose one and share your appreciation report.

- Title of your report
- Information on the reporter (name, affiliation, grade, etc.)
- Facts about the topic you are reporting (who, when, where, etc.)
- A brief summary of the event/story
- Highlights of the event/story
- Overall rating, star rating (1-5), what score would you give and why?
- Your feelings about it
- Things you like/dislike about it, and why?
- For the closing remark, what do you want to tell your readers?

Writing Tips

 쓰기 과정 계획하기
Planning Your Writing

In writing, going through an outline process is helpful, especially to beginner-level language learners, because it encourages communication through writing despite limited understanding of structure.

As you start writing about simple personal reports, as in this lesson, consider the suggested process:

- Outlining (brainstorming, selecting ideas)
- Prewriting (making simple notes using keywords, phrases, and simple sentences)
- Drafting (putting the information in sentences using connectives, conjunctions, etc.)
- Revising (reviewing and getting comments from other people)
- Editing (proofreading, checking on grammar/spelling)
- Writing the Final Draft

 인용 부호: 큰따옴표 (" ") vs 작은따옴표 (' ')
Quotation Marks

큰따옴표 " " is used to indicate conversations (dialogues) or direct quotes.

ex 봉준호 감독은 "가장 개인적인 것이 가장 창의적인 것"이라는 말을 한 스콜세지 감독을 가리켰다.

작은따옴표 ' ' is used to indicate that it is a quote in a direct quote or a word/phrase/sentence in one's thoughts. It is also used to indicate the title of a book, movie, song, drama, event, and art piece.

ex 봉준호 감독의 영화 '기생충', 방탄소년단의 '다이너마이트'

감상 후기 쓰기
Writing a Review Essay

There are various review essay topics, such as film, music, story, book, poetry, etc. Review essays generally comprise four sections:

1. Introduction: Write a brief introduction, such as the reason/ background for choosing the topic.

2. Summary: Write the plot/summary and general information about your topic.

3. Your reviews and discussion: Write your topic's most impressive part and highlights, providing more examples and explanations. You may focus on characters, lyrics, scenes, script lines, etc.

4. Conclusion: It is crucial to include your overall thoughts and feelings about the topic.

In your review essay, it is essential to include your reflection on the topic, including your thoughts, experiences, feelings, what you have learned, opinions, etc.

4.5. | 여행 후기 Reviewing Trips

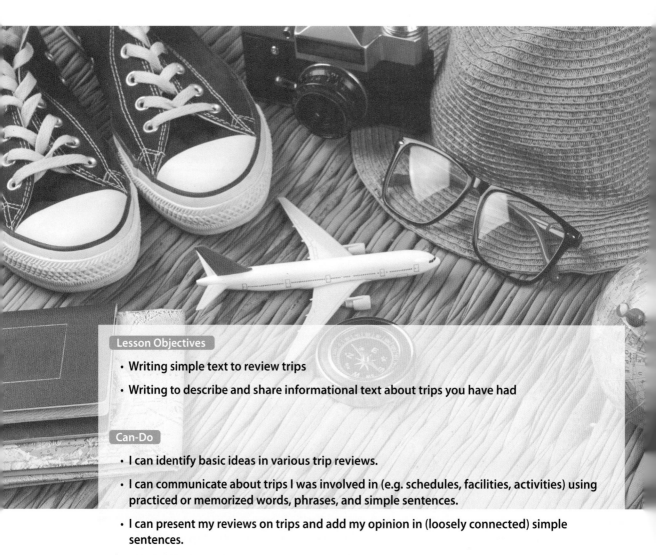

Lesson Objectives

- Writing simple text to review trips
- Writing to describe and share informational text about trips you have had

Can-Do

- I can identify basic ideas in various trip reviews.
- I can communicate about trips I was involved in (e.g. schedules, facilities, activities) using practiced or memorized words, phrases, and simple sentences.
- I can present my reviews on trips and add my opinion in (loosely connected) simple sentences.

 Useful Vocabulary, Grammar, and Expressions

1. Vocabulary

(1) ☐ 여행 trip   ☐ 장소 place   ☐ 계획 plan

☐ 일정(표) itinerary   ☐ 자전거 bicycle   ☐ (자동)차 car

☐ 버스 bus   ☐ 지하철 subway   ☐ 기차 train

☐ 비행기 airplane   ☐ 역 station   ☐ 공항 airport

국내선 domestic lines   국제선 international lines   여행사 travel agency

표 ticket   여행지 travel destination   관광지 tourist attraction

관광객 tourist   숙박 lodging   지도 map

기념품 souvenir   맛집 gourmet restaurant   1박 2일 1 night & 2 days stay

(2) 볼거리(=볼 것) things to see   할거리(=할 것) things to do   놀거리(=놀 것) things to play

먹(을)거리(=먹을 것) things to eat   살거리(=살 것) things to buy

(3) 걷다 to walk   걸어 다니다 to walk around   타다 to ride

사다 to buy   예약하다 to make a reservation   여행하다 to travel

방문하다 to visit   관광하다 to go sightseeing   구경하다 to see

2. Grammar

① -아/어 보다 to try to

② -아/어 본 적이 있다/없다 to have/not have experienced to

③ -고 싶다/싶어 하다 to want to

④ -아/어 보고 싶다/싶어 하다 to want to try to

⑤ -았/었으면 좋겠다 to be great if I could

⑥ -고 and, -고 (나서) after -ing and

⑦ -지만 however

⑧ -(으)ㄴ데/는데 and/but (giving background information)

⑨ -기 때문에, -아/어서, -(으)니까 because

⑩ N(vehicle)(으)로 number + 시간/분(쯤) 걸려요. It takes # hours/minutes by N(vehicle)

3. Expressions

① 여기/거기 가 봤어요? Have you been here/there?

② 한번 가 보세요. Please give it a try (to go).

③ 가볼 만해요. It's worth a try (to go).

④ 어때요/어땠어요? How is/was it?

⑤ 어떤 할거리/볼거리/먹거리가 있어요? What kind of things to do/see/eat?

⑥ 어디(에) 꼭 가봐야 돼요? Where should I visit for sure?

⑦ 어디(에)서 뭐(를) 하면 좋아요? Where and what should I do?

⑧ 얼마 들었어요? How much did it cost?

Writing Samples

1. Joyce and her roommates are planning a summer vacation trip together. They read advertisements and reviews about local activities that are listed on a travel review site.

하늘을 날다 "번지 점프"

1회: 5만 원
안전 보장
초보자 환영 (교육 포함)

후기

- 좀 무섭지만 재미있었어요!
- 꼭 한번 해 보세요^^
- 내 버킷 리스트 #1 성공!!!

하늘 sky, 날다 to fly, 안전 safety, 보장 guaranteed, 초보자 novice, 교육 training, 포함 included, 성공 success

물을 가르다 "수상 스키"

1회: 7만 5천 원
초급, 중급, 고급 코스
초보자 환영 (안전요원 있음)

후기

- 스피드를 좋아한다면 강추!
- 물이 좀 차가웠지만...
- 정말 재밌었어요. 또 하고 싶어요.

가르다 to divide, 수상 스키 water skiing 초/중/고급 novice/intermediate/advanced level, 안전요원 safety guard, 차갑다 to be cold

자연을 찾다 "정글 탐험"

1회: 20만 원 (가이드 포함)
오전 10시 – 오후 5시
3–5명/그룹

후기

- 신기한 동물, 식물들이 많아요!
- 가이드가 친절하고 좋았어요.
- 긴 옷이랑 모자 꼭 가져 가세요!

자연 nature, 찾다 to search, 탐험 exploration, 신기한 unusual, 동물 animal, 식물 plant

2. Paul and Jane are searching for a travel package for their honeymoon. They found a travel agency site where newlywed couples posted their honest reviews.

여행나라 신혼 패키지 후기

제주도에서 3박 4일 보내기 (shinhon237)

- 호텔이 공항에서 가까워서 편했어요. 그리고 깨끗해요.
- 가이드가 정말 친절했어요. 김지민 가이드님 최고!!!
- 다른 여행사에 비해 좀 비싼 편. (그렇지만 여행 내용이 좋음)
- 음식이 더 다양했으면 좋겠어요. 제주도 "진짜" 음식 먹고 싶었는데 ㅠㅠ
- 스케줄이 좀 빡빡해서 헉헉...

우리의 꿈 하와이 1주일 패키지 (Igotmarried!!)

- 하와이 너무 멀다 ㅠㅠ
- 스케줄을 마음대로 바꿀 수 없어서 비추.
- 음식이나 숙박은 괜찮았음
- 신혼 그룹이라 재미있었는데 개인 시간이 별로 없었음 (쇼핑 못 했어, 엉엉)
- 추가 관광이나 액티비티에 돈이 많이 들었어요.

유럽 9박 10일 생생 후기 (taken2022)

- 비행기가 밤에 도착해서 좀 피곤했어요.
- 가이드가 설명을 잘 해 주시고 사진도 찍어 주셔서 좋았어요. (팁 많이 드림 ^^)
- 아침 일찍 일어나는 스케줄이라서 힘들지만 많이 구경할 수 있어요.
- 9박10일 패키지보다는 13박14일 패키지를 추천합니다.

제주도 Jeju Island, 3박4일 three nights four days, 최고 the best, —에 비해 compared to, 편 side, 내용 content, 다양하다 various, 빡빡하다 tight, 헉헉 heavy breathing sound, 마음대로 as wish, 비추 not recommended, 숙박 lodging, 신혼 newlywed, 추가 additional, 들다 to cost, 도착하다 to arrive, 설명 explanation, —보다 rather than, 추천하다 to recommend, 생생 vivid

Pre-Writing Exercises

1. For summer vacation, you and your family rented a house via Airbnb in Jeju Island in Korea (or Hawaii if you have no idea about Jeju). It was a wonderful stay and you want to write a review for the property.

❶ First, list things in Korean about the house.

- Location/Address (위치/주소) ....

- Price (가격) ....

- # of rooms (방 개수): ....

- Size (크기): ....

- Cleanness (청결도): ....

- Facility/Amenities (시설/비품): 침대/책상/소파/식탁/그릇/수건/샴푸/비누/세탁기/에어컨/인터넷 등

  ....

- Anything else (기타)

  ....

❷ Next, list things in Korean that you and your family did/visited/ate at the house or near the

area. (ex) 할거리, 볼거리, 먹(을)거리

- ....
- ....
- ....

❸ List things you liked/disliked while staying there.

- ....
- ....
- ....

❹ List things to improve.

- ....
- ....
- ....

❺ Using your lists above, write a review to describe your experience.

지난 여름 방학에 가족들과 함께 제주도 (or 하와이)에 갔어요. 우리는 음식을 만들어 먹고 싶었기 때문에 호텔 대신에 에어비앤비에서 집을 빌렸어요.

다음에 이곳에 또 가고 싶어요. 강추합니다!!!

대신(에) instead of, 빌리다 to rent

Interpersonal Writing

1. As a member of the Graduation Field Trip Committee of the Korean class at San Jose High School, you sent a survey to graduated seniors who have been on the trip before. Based on their replies below, ask additional questions about their trips in detail so that the committee can use the information for deciding where to go and what to do.

(1) From Wangwei

To. 산호세 고등학교 한국어반 졸업여행 준비위원회

우리 반은 2년 전에 1박 2일로 샌프란시스코에 갔어요.
금문교(Golden Gate Bridge)도 보고 Pier 39에서 게도 먹었어요.
짧은 여행이었지만 아주 재미있었습니다!

From. 왕웨이

REPLY

준비 preparation, 위원회 committee, 게 crab, 짧은 short

(2) From Salina

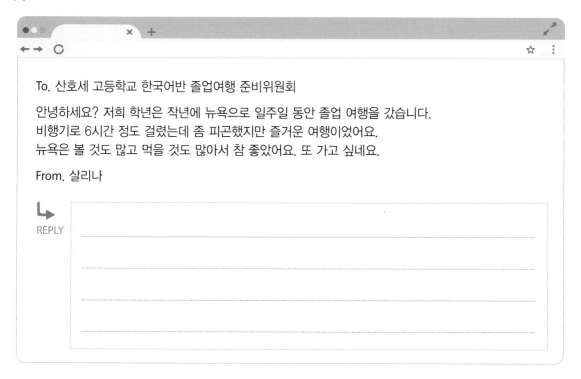

To. 산호세 고등학교 한국어반 졸업여행 준비위원회

안녕하세요? 저희 학년은 작년에 뉴욕으로 일주일 동안 졸업 여행을 갔습니다.
비행기로 6시간 정도 걸렸는데 좀 피곤했지만 즐거운 여행이었어요.
뉴욕은 볼 것도 많고 먹을 것도 많아서 참 좋았어요. 또 가고 싶네요.

From. 살리나

REPLY

(3) From Junko

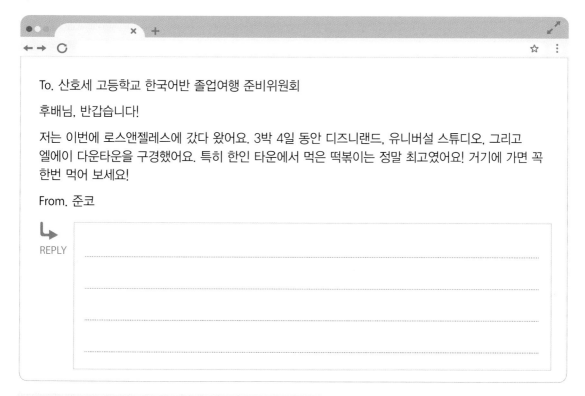

To. 산호세 고등학교 한국어반 졸업여행 준비위원회

후배님, 반갑습니다!

저는 이번에 로스앤젤레스에 갔다 왔어요. 3박 4일 동안 디즈니랜드, 유니버설 스튜디오, 그리고
엘에이 다운타운을 구경했어요. 특히 한인 타운에서 먹은 떡볶이는 정말 최고였어요! 거기에 가면 꼭
한번 먹어 보세요!

From. 준코

REPLY

후배 junior, 한인 타운 Korea Town, 특히 particularly, 최고 the best

Presentational Writing

1. You are writing a travel review for a special edition of the travel magazine *Travel Sketch*. Choose your most memorable trip and write in detail.

   (1) What is your most memorable travel destination?

   Q: 가장 기억에 남는 여행지는 어디예요?

   A: _____

   기억에 남다 to be memorable, 여행지 destination

   (2) What was the travel itinerary for your trip?

   여행 일정표

(3) Write a review about the trip. You can include your experience about the number of days, transportation, places stayed at/visited, activities, food you tried, etc.

나의 가장 기억에 남는 여행

(4) Based on your experience above, write a suggestion for readers who want to visit the same place.

Writing Tips

표지판 읽기
Reading Signs

1. In Korea, most official signs of tourist attraction are written in both Korean and English. Please refer to the site below regarding the Romanization of Korean.

   https://www.korean.go.kr/front_eng/roman/roman_01.do

2. As a macro-to-micro language, Korean starts from a larger unit then proceeds to a smaller unit. For example, you will find addresses and street signs written in the order of country-province-city-street-house number.

   `ex` 대한민국 경기도 일산시 서구 주엽동 32번지

   Likewise, dates are written in the order of year-month-day.

   `ex` 2025년 12월 25일

여행 후기 쓰기
Writing Travel Reviews

Here's a simple and brief guide to organizing your travel review:

1. Destination: Start with the name of the place you visited.

2. Duration: Mention how long your trip was.

3. Highlights: List famous sites or attractions you visited.

4. Activities: Share what you enjoyed doing.

5. Accommodation: Describe where you stayed.

6. Budget: Provide an overview of your travel expenses.

7. Cuisine: Talk about the local food and drinks you tried.

8. Transportation: Describe how you got around, including any tips on public transport or car rentals.

Lesson Objectives

- Writing simple opinion statements and comments
- Writing to present and exchange simple personal opinions (for or against) with simple reasons (pros and cons) on familiar daily topics

Can-Do

- I can recognize basic words, phrases, visual symbols, and expressions on voting or a poll to decide pros and cons.
- I can ask and express briefly about personal opinions (for/against) on familiar topics using a series of simple sentences and basic connectives.
- I can provide simple reasons (pros and cons/strengths and weaknesses) to support my opinion using learned vocabulary, phrases, expressions, and simple sentences.

Useful Vocabulary, Grammar, and Expressions

1. Vocabulary

(1) ☐ 찬성 for   ☐ 반대 against   ☐ 장점 pros

☐ 단점 cons   ☐ 장단점 pros and cons   ☐ 강점 strength

☐ 약점 weakness   ☐ 의견 opinion   ☐ 생각 thought

☐ 결론 conclusion

(2) ☐ 동의하다 to agree   ☐ 반대하다 to be against   ☐ 투표하다 to vote

      ☐ 결정하다 to make a decision   ☐ 선택하다 to choose/select

(3) ☐ 그러나/그렇지만 however   ☐ 그래도 nevertheless   ☐ 그러므로 therefore

      ☐ 반면(에) on the other hand   ☐ 결론적으로 in conclusion

(4) ☐ 제 생각에는 in my opinion

2. Grammar

① -다고 생각하다 I think that

② -(으)ㄴ/는/(으)ㄹ 것 같다 I think

③ -(으)면 안 되다 it is not allowed

④ -아/어도 괜찮다/되다 it is ok/allowed

3. Expressions

① 어떻게 생각하세요? What do you think?

② 왜 그렇게 생각하세요? Why do you think so?

③ 의견을 말씀해 주세요. Please share your opinion.

Writing Samples

1. Yulia loves listening to the Korean radio talk show, Your Voice (너의 목소리). Every week, the host selects some comments the audience submits to add their voices to the show's weekly topic. This week's topic is "Can singers lip-sync in their concerts?" (가수들이 콘서트에서 립싱크해도 괜찮아요?).

   Here is Yulia's opinion she posted.

   Yulia

   > 저는 찬성해요.
   > 그 이유는, 가수들은 콘서트에서 노래하면서 춤도 많이 춰요.
   > 그런데 춤추면서 노래하는 것은 힘들어요. 그래서 춤에 집중할 수 없다고 생각해요.
   > 그래서 립싱크는 빠르고 춤이 많이 있을 때 꼭 필요해요.
   > 하지만 발라드처럼 조용하고 느린 노래를 부를 때는 립싱크가 필요 없어요.
   > 결론적으로, 립싱크는 빠르고 춤이 많을 때 필요해요.

   MJ

   > 반대!!!
   > 저는 립싱크 반대해요.
   > 가수들은 노래를 잘 해야 돼요. 제 생각에는, 춤만 잘 추면 진짜 가수가 아니에요. 팬들은 가수하고 라이브 공연을 보고 싶어서 표를 사요. 그리고 보통 콘서트 표가 아주 비싸요.
   > 저는 가수가 콘서트에서 립싱크하면 안 갈 거예요.
   > 그래서 가수들은 콘서트에서 립싱크를 하면 안 돼요.

   필요없다 to not need, 집중하다 to focus/concentrate, 라이브 공연 live performance

2. Sooho is a rising junior in college. He lived in a dormitory on campus for two years, but he plans to live with his friends in an off-campus apartment in his junior year. He noted down the pros and cons of off-campus living to justify his preference to his parents.

   장점
   1. 요리할 수 있어요.
   2. 먹고 싶을 때 먹을 수 있어요.
   3. 기숙사보다 싸요.
   4. 친한 친구들하고 살 수 있어요.
   5. 방을 혼자 사용해요.
   6. 졸업 후의 생활을 연습해요.
   7. 친구들을 초대할 수 있어요.

   단점
   1. 학교까지 15분 쯤 걸어야 돼요.
   2. 화장실 청소도 하고 쓰레기도 버려야 돼요.
   3. 설거지 해야 돼요.
   4. 매달 월세, 전기세를 내야 돼요.

   설거지하다 to wash dishes, 월세 monthly rent, 전기세 electricity bill

Pre-Writing Exercises

1. You and your friends are going to have a sleepover and watch a movie this weekend. Respond to your friend's text message.

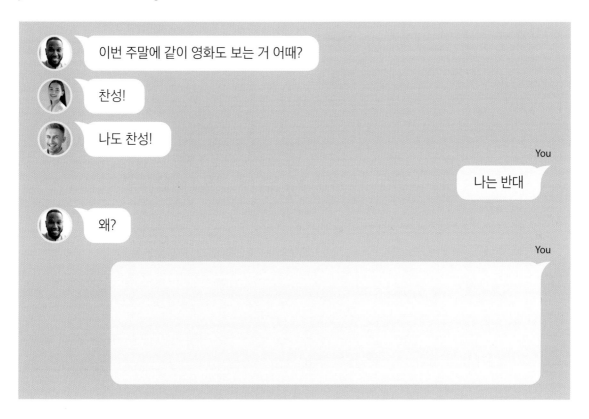

2. Your hobby club is planning to host its spring picnic at the local park. The event organizer posted a poll on the group chat platform to ask the members' preferences for the lunch menu for the event.

(1) Vote for your preferences.

선호하다 to prefer, 투표하다 to vote

(2) The voting result came out that two choices are tied. The event organizer posted a follow-up question to collect the members' input.

점심 도시락 메뉴

1. 어느 것을 선호하세요?

투표 결과

김밥	16
샌드위치	16

그럼, 점심 메뉴로 김밥이나 샌드위치의 좋은 점과 나쁜 점을 편하게 말해 주세요.

감사합니다.

김밥

좋은 점	나쁜 점
○	○
○	○
○	○

샌드위치

좋은 점	나쁜 점
○	○
○	○
○	○

-(으)로 for

Interpersonal Writing

1. Your office colleague's birthday is approaching, and your team is planning to give a birthday gift together. What do you think about one of the gift ideas suggested, and why do you agree or disagree?

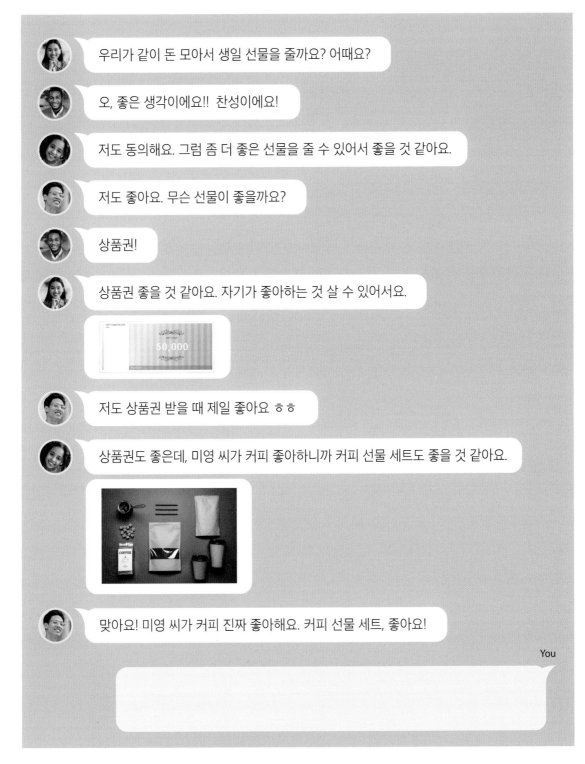

2. The Student Council of your school has posted a petition on the student community site to seek students' opinions. Participate in the petition to add your voice.

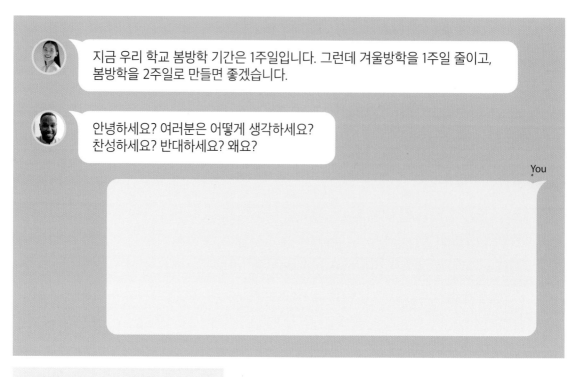

지금 우리 학교 봄방학 기간은 1주일입니다. 그런데 겨울방학을 1주일 줄이고, 봄방학을 2주일로 만들면 좋겠습니다.

안녕하세요? 여러분은 어떻게 생각하세요?
찬성하세요? 반대하세요? 왜요?

You

기간 time duration, period, 줄이다 to shorten

Presentational Writing

1. You are an international student in Korea and decided to live with four other friends in an off-campus apartment this summer.

   (1) One of your roommates initiated a discussion poll about the following household rules. Do you agree or disagree on each rule, and why?

#1. 집 안에서는 신발을 안 신는다.　　　　☐ 찬성　　　반대

이유: _____

_____

#2. 화장실 청소는 주말마다 한다.　　　　찬성　　　반대

이유: _____

_____

#3. 쓰레기는 일주일에 세 번 버린다.　　　　찬성　　　반대

이유: _____

_____

#4. 친구들을 초대할 때는 미리 알려준다.　　　　찬성　　　반대

이유: _____

_____

#5. 밖에 나갈 때는 불을 항상 끈다.　　　　찬성　　　반대

이유: _____

_____

쓰레기를 버리다 to take out the trash, 미리 in advance, 끄다 to turn off

(2) Now, you further develop your opinion by elaborating and adding more concrete examples. Consider taking the guided step-by-step process. These may help you in processing your thoughts and writing with ease.

- Choose one household rule from #1-5 above.
- Think about the pros and cons and list them.
- Write your final thought or opinion.

The subject/topic

....

....

Your opinion   ☐ 찬성   ☐ 반대

Pros and Cons

좋은 점	안 좋은 점
◦ 첫째,	◦
◦ 둘째,	◦
◦ 셋째,	◦

Conclusion

1) ....

2) 저는 찬성/반대해요. ....

3) 좋은 점은 ....

   ....

   안 좋은 점은 ....

   ....

4) 그래서 ....

Writing Tips

 제안/주장하는 글쓰기
Writing Argumentative Essays

An argumentative essay is a type of writing that presents a clear position on a topic and uses evidence and reasoning to support that position. When writing an argumentative essay, there are two common approaches that you can take:

1. Agree or disagree (찬성 반대 주장):
   In this approach, you take a clear position on a topic and argue either for or against it. Your goal is to persuade the reader that your position is the correct one. Explain your perspective; for example, present reasons to support your argument (pros and cons, suggesting solutions to solve a problem.)

2. Problem-solving/solutions (문제해결 제안):
   In this approach, you identify a problem or issue and suggest solutions. Your goal is to convince readers that your solutions are feasible and effective. Make suggestions to solve the issue or problem.

Regardless of the approach you choose, here are some tips for writing an effective argumentative essay:

1. Introduction: Introduce the problem:
   Your thesis statement should clearly state your position or proposed solutions and preview the main points you will use to support your argument.

2. Body:
   Present your main position (either you agree or disagree with reasons; suggest your solutions)

3. Conclusion:
   Conclude your argument. Sum up your argument and restate your thesis. Leave the reader with a final thought or call to action.

Your writing should be clear, concise, and easy to follow. Use transition words to connect your ideas and improve the flow of your essay.

5.2. | 조언 Advice

Lesson Objectives

- Writing simple text to advise someone
- Writing to describe and share advice you have given or received

Can-Do

- I can understand the basic messages of various pieces of personal advice on familiar topics.
- I can exchange basic information to communicate about advice I gave/received using practiced or memorized words, phrases, and simple sentences.
- I can provide, in writing, my personal advice on familiar daily topics using simple sentences and connectives.

 Useful Vocabulary, Grammar, and Expressions

1. Vocabulary

(1) ☐ 고민 concern   ☐ 걱정 worry   ☐ 조언 advice

     ☐ 도움말 helpful remarks   ☐ 의견 opinion

(2)   ☐ 얘기하다 to talk to   ☐ 들어 주다 to listen to   ☐ 도와주다 to help

     ☐ 의논하다 to discuss   ☐ 상담하다 to counsel   ☐ 마음을 터놓다 to open one's heart to

     ☐ 스트레스를 받다 / 스트레스가 쌓이다 to get stressed   ☐ 속상하다 to upset

     ☐ 화나다 to get angry   ☐ 슬프다 to be sad   ☐ 힘들다 to be arduous

2. Grammar

① -어/아야 하다/되다 should

② -기 -ing

③ -는 게 (더) 좋겠어요 It would be better to, -(으)면 좋겠어요 it would be good if

④ -(으)면 어때요/어떨까요? How about if

3. Expressions

① 어떻게 (해야) 할까요/될까요? What should I do?

② 다시 한번 생각해 보세요. Please consider it again.

③ 잘 생각했어요. You made a right decision.

④ 좋은 생각이에요. That's a good idea.

⑤ 너무 걱정하지 마세요. Don't worry too much.

⑥ 조언해 주셔서 감사합니다. Thanks for your advice.

Writing Samples

1. Hankook University made a poll asking seniors to choose one thing first-year students should do during their college life. The top ten list was recently posted in the welcoming packet for freshmen.

"새내기 대학생? 이것만은 꼭!!!"
선배들이 조언하는 대학 생활 버킷 리스트 10

1. 미팅, 소개팅은 대학 생활의 필수!
2. 동아리 적어도 한 개는 꼭 해야 돼요!
3. 선배들과 친하게 지내세요. 밥은 늘 공짜 ^^
4. 교환학생 프로그램에 참여해 보세요~
5. 남자/여자 친구 꼭 만나기를... 화이팅!!!
6. 나 홀로 배낭 여행!
7. 첫눈 오는 날 데이트 하기
8. All A 받아서 장학금 받으면 좋겠지요?
9. 자격증은 많을수록 좋습니다. 미리 미리 준비하세요.
10. 술 마시기, 연애하기, 밤새워 공부하기...다 해 봐요!

미팅/소개팅 blind date, 필수 required, 동아리 club, 적어도 at least, 공짜 for free, 교환학생 exchange student, 홀로 alone, 배낭 여행 backpacking, 장학금 scholarship, 자격증 certificate, ―(으)ㄹ수록 the more, 미리 in advance, 연애 dating, 밤새우다 staying up all night

2. "South Korean Foreigners (대한 외국인)" is a popular TV program in Korea featuring foreigners who can speak Korean very well. People were amazed by their fluency and asked how they became fluent speakers.

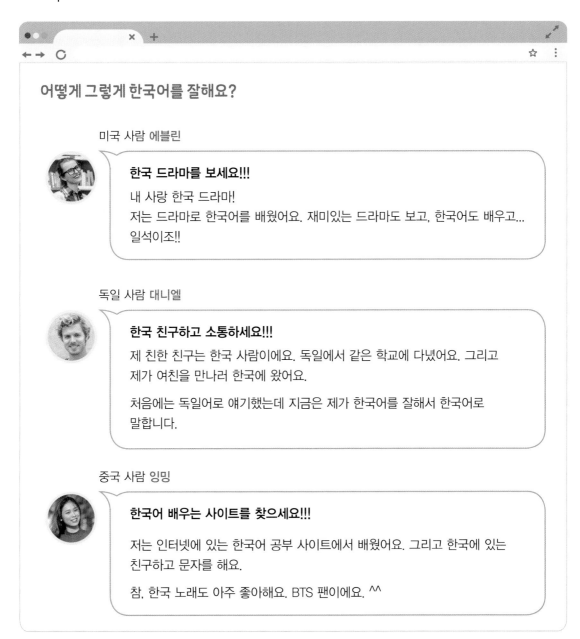

어떻게 그렇게 한국어를 잘해요?

미국 사람 에블린

한국 드라마를 보세요!!!
내 사랑 한국 드라마!
저는 드라마로 한국어를 배웠어요. 재미있는 드라마도 보고, 한국어도 배우고...
일석이조!!

독일 사람 대니엘

한국 친구하고 소통하세요!!!
제 친한 친구는 한국 사람이에요. 독일에서 같은 학교에 다녔어요. 그리고 제가 여친을 만나러 한국에 왔어요.

처음에는 독일어로 얘기했는데 지금은 제가 한국어를 잘해서 한국어로 말합니다.

중국 사람 잉밍

한국어 배우는 사이트를 찾으세요!!!
저는 인터넷에 있는 한국어 공부 사이트에서 배웠어요. 그리고 한국에 있는 친구하고 문자를 해요.

참, 한국 노래도 아주 좋아해요. BTS 팬이에요. ^^

일석이조 Killing two birds with one stone

Pre-Writing Exercises

1. You realize that something is going on with your friends. Check it out and give them appropriate advice.

❶

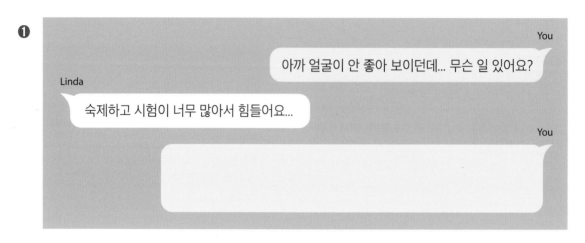

You

아까 얼굴이 안 좋아 보이던데... 무슨 일 있어요?

Linda

숙제하고 시험이 너무 많아서 힘들어요...

You

❷

You

어디 아파요?

Jason

눈이 좀 아프네요. SNS를 너무 많이 했어요 ㅠㅠ

You

❸

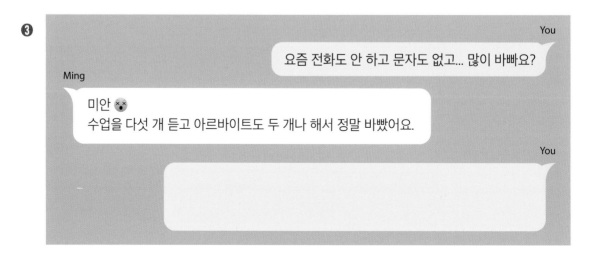

You

요즘 전화도 안 하고 문자도 없고... 많이 바빠요?

Ming

미안 😵
수업을 다섯 개 듣고 아르바이트도 두 개나 해서 정말 바빴어요.

You

2. You are a college freshman and need to buy a new computer. You cannot decide whether you should buy a laptop or a desktop. You know that laptops are easier to carry around. However, as a game maniac, you also want to have a powerful desktop. Send a text message to your senior at the Computer Club and ask which one you should buy.

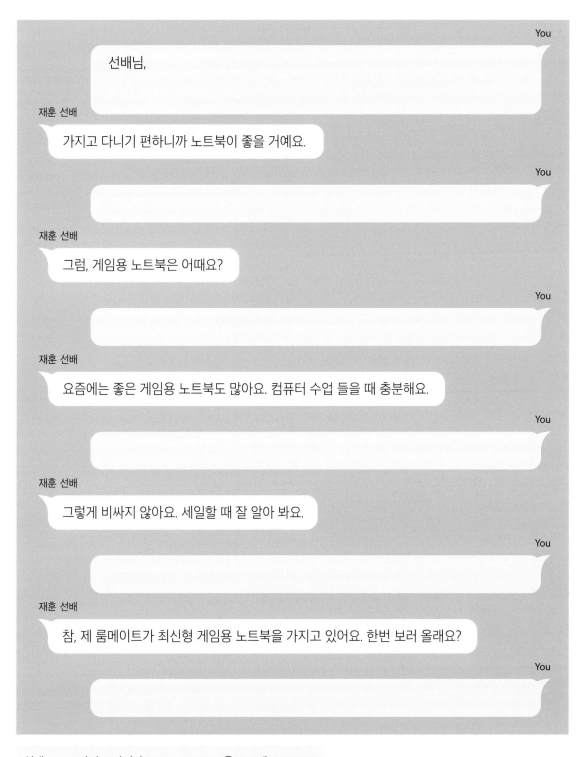

선배님,

재훈 선배
가지고 다니기 편하니까 노트북이 좋을 거예요.

재훈 선배
그럼, 게임용 노트북은 어때요?

재훈 선배
요즘에는 좋은 게임용 노트북도 많아요. 컴퓨터 수업 들을 때 충분해요.

재훈 선배
그렇게 비싸지 않아요. 세일할 때 잘 알아 봐요.

재훈 선배
참, 제 룸메이트가 최신형 게임용 노트북을 가지고 있어요. 한번 보러 올래요?

선배 senior, 가지고 다니다 to carry around, ─용 use, 때 time when,
충분하다 to be enough, 최신형 the latest model, 노트북 laptop

Interpersonal Writing

1. You are a counselor who runs an advice column 오 박사에게 물어 보세요 (Ask Dr. Oh) in a
newspaper in Korea. Reply to the readers who sent messages asking for your advice.

(1) From Jinsuh

오 박사님,

저는 내년에 대학교에 가야 하는 고3인데, 공부하기가 너~무 싫어요.
어떻게 하면 좋을까요?
김진서

Dr. Oh's Advice

(2) From Yumi

오 박사님께

짝사랑하는 남자애가 제 가장 친구 현지하고 사귀게 됐어요.
축하해 줘야 하는데... 그게 잘 안 되네요. ㅠㅠ 박사님 생각은 어떠세요? 저 좀 도와 주세요.
정유미 드림

Dr. Oh's Advice

(3) From Yoojin

오 선생님,

룸메이트가 집안일을 너무 안 해요. 그래서 지난주에 룸메이트하고 싸웠어요.
일주일 동안 말도 안 했어요. 저...정말 힘들어요. 어떻게 해요? ㅠㅠ
유진 올림

Dr. Oh's Advice

Presentational Writing

1. Your friend Emily called you last night and talked about her dilemma in deciding which major she will pursue. She likes math but is not good at it. She likes to study music but is not sure what to do after graduation. Emily's mom wants her to study biology and become a doctor. It may be good, but she is rather interested in becoming a teacher.

   After talking with Emily over the phone last night, you thought about her dilemma and decided to write an email now to give her some advice.

수학 mathematics, 음악 music, 생물학 biology

2. You are a professor at a college in Korea. As a freshman advisor this year, you are invited to give a talk at a welcome orientation about how to choose one's major. What kind of advice can you give them? Make a short paragraph summarizing your talk.

이유 설명하기: ─아/어서, ─(으)니까, ─기 때문에

Explaining Reasons

-아/어서, -(으)니까, -기 때문에 can be all translated to "because" but there is a slight difference in how each expression sounds. Please note that there is a certain restriction in using them.

First, -아/어서 cannot be used with tense, which is different from -(으)니까, -기 때문에

ex 늦게 일어났어서 아침을 못 먹었어요. (X)

→ 늦게 일어나서 아침을 못 먹었어요.

늦게 일어났으니까 아침을 못 먹었어요.

늦게 일어났기 때문에 아침을 못 먹었어요.

Second, -아/어서 and -기 때문에 cannot be used with command or suggestion.

ex 추워서 옷을 더 입으세요. (X)

춥기 때문에 옷을 더 입으세요. (X)

→ 추우니까 옷을 더 입으세요.

5.3. | 주장과 제안 Argument and Suggestion

Lesson Objectives

- Writing simple argumentative comments
- Writing to present and exchange simple argumentative opinions and make suggestions with simple reasons on highly familiar topics

Can-Do

- I can recognize simple text organization of assertions/insistences/suggestions recognizing words, phrases, expressions, and simple sentences I learned and practiced.
- I can communicate briefly about one's/my opinions and make suggestions on familiar topics using simple sentences and connectives.
- I can provide simple reasons to support my arguments/suggestions in sentences.

Useful Vocabulary, Grammar, and Expressions

1. Vocabulary

(1) ☐ 이유 reasons   ☐ 의견 opinion   ☐ 경험 experience

    ☐ 제안하다 to suggest   ☐ 주장하다 to insist

(2) ☐ 첫째/첫 번째 first   ☐ 둘째/두 번째 second   ☐ 셋째/세 번째 third

    ☐ 넷째/네 번째 fourth

(3) ☐ 그러므로/그래서 therefore   ☐ 그런데/하지만/그러나 but, however   ☐ 물론 of course

2. Grammar

① -아/어 보는 게 어때요?/ -아/어 보는 건 어떨까요? How about trying?

② -아/어 보세요 Please try -ing, -아/어 보는 것도 좋을 것 같다 I think that you want to do…

③ -아/어 보기 바라다 I hope/suggest you try

④ -는 것을 제안하다 I suggest that

⑤ 그 이유는/ 왜냐하면 -기 때문이다 the reason is because

⑥ -다고 생각하다 I think that

3. Expressions

① 예를 들면 for example

② 뿐만 아니라 as well as

③ 제 생각에는 in my opinion

④ 어떻게 하면 좋을까요? What shall I do?

⑤ 좋은 생각이 있으면 제안해 주시기 바랍니다. Please make suggestions if you have any good ideas.

⑥ 제안해 주실래요? Would you please suggest (your opinion)?

⑦ 제안해 주셔서 감사합니다. Thank you for your suggestion.

⑧ 어때요? How about this?

⑨ 어떻게 생각해요/생각하세요? What do you think?

⑩ 편하게 의견을 알려 주시기 바랍니다. Please feel free to let us know your thoughts.

Writing Samples

1. Willow is a Korean American senior at a college and a residential counselor for a group of first-year students. Grace, one of her group members who is also a Korean American, just texted Willow about her problem. Willow responded to Grace with her suggestion.

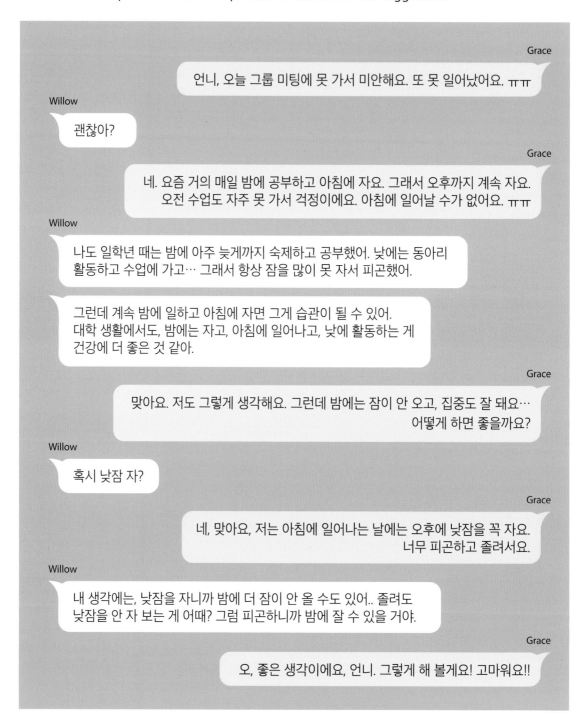

습관 habit, 집중이 잘 되다 to be easy to focus/concentrate, 낮잠 자다 to take a nap

2. Ahmed is a student at Hankuk University, and this year, he serves as president of a student K-Pop dance club, Connection (커넥션).

The Connection's board members discussed its audition process and requirements. Here is the summary of their agreed suggestions and supporting arguments Ahmed wrote for the club members for further discussion and approval.

커넥션 회원 여러분, 안녕하세요?

우리 동아리 커넥션을 오디션이 없는 동아리로 바꾸는 것을 제안합니다.

물론, 오디션이 있으면 좋은 점도 있습니다.

첫째, 우리 대학교 댄스 동아리들도 다 오디션이 있습니다.

둘째, 오디션이 있으면 춤을 잘 추는 회원들을 뽑을 수 있습니다.

하지만, 오디션이 있어서 안 좋은 점도 많습니다.

첫째, 우리 동아리는 취미 동아리입니다. 대학 생활에서 우리들은 바쁘고 스트레스도 많이 받습니다. 그래서 관심이 있고 하고 싶으면 누구나 동아리에 가입할 수 있어야 됩니다.

둘째, 오디션이 1차, 2차 있어서 동아리에 가입하기가 너무 어렵습니다. 그래서 전공이 춤이 아닌 학생들은 오디션이 무섭고 스트레스를 더 받을 수 있습니다.

셋째, 우리 동아리의 목적은 K-Pop 댄스에 관심이 있는 학생들이 같이 배우고, 가르쳐 주고, 즐기면서 친해지는 것입니다. 그리고 친구들하고 편하고 재미있게 춤을 출 수 있어야 됩니다. 그런데 우리 동아리에 가입하려면 경쟁을 많이 해야 됩니다. 동아리에 가입하기 위해서 경쟁하는 것은 정신 건강에 좋지 않습니다.

그래서, 오디션을 하지 않고, 우리 동아리에 관심이 있고 같이 활동하고 싶은 학생들 모두 환영하는 것을 제안합니다.

회원 여러분은 어떻게 생각하세요? 편하게 의견을 알려 주시기 바랍니다.

목적 purpose, 경쟁 competition, 정신 건강 mental health, 오디션 audition

Pre-Writing Exercises

1. You are a member of the student council at your college. Every month, the student council has a meeting, and each council member brings problems and suggestions to benefit the entire student body of the school.

   (1) Make notes on problematic situations in your school you want to address in the meeting. (Write in sentences.)

#1

학교 식당 메뉴가 더 다양하면 좋겠어요.

#2

#3

#4

#5

#6

2. Now, you are preparing to add supporting ideas to your suggestion, such as examples or reasons. List 2 to 3 reasons in simple sentences.

#1
제안: 학교 식당 메뉴가 더 다양하면 좋겠어요.

이유: 첫째, 학생들이 아침을 보통 많이 안 먹습니다. 그런데, 점심에도 아침 식사 메뉴가 있으면 좋아하는 아침을 먹을 수 있습니다.

둘째, 우리 학교에는 아시안 학생들도 많이 있어서, 그 학생들이 좋아하는 음식들도 학교 식당 메뉴에 더하면 우리 학교 학생들이 다양한 문화의 음식을 경험할 수 있다고 생각합니다.

셋째, 따뜻한 수프나 라면처럼 국물이 있는 음식이 있으면, 날씨가 추울 때, 아플 때에도 학생들이 엄마 음식처럼 먹을 수 있을 것 같습니다.

#2
제안: 주말에 도서관 이용 시간이 평일하고 같아야 돼요.

이유: 첫째, 토요일하고 일요일에도 숙제하거나 시험 공부를 할 수 있어요.

둘째, 기숙사에서 집중할 수 없는 학생들은 도서관에서 공부해야 돼요.

셋째, 주말 오후에 보통 동아리 활동을 하고 나서, 저녁이나 밤에 공부할 수 있습니다.

집중하다 to concentrate

#3
제안:

이유: 첫째,

둘째,

셋째,

#4
제안:

이유: 첫째,

  둘째,

  셋째,

#5
제안:

이유: 첫째,

  둘째,

  셋째,

#6
제안:

이유: 첫째,

  둘째,

  셋째,

Interpersonal Writing

1. Your volunteer service group is planning to host a fundraising event for the organization. The event organizer sent the team members an email seeking fundraising ideas. As a member of the team, reply with your opinion. In your reply, include your argument, reasons, and suggestions in simple sentences.

보내는사람   조미수@mansei.com

받는 사람

제목   모금 아이디어

안녕하세요?

올해에도 모금 행사를 하려고 하는데요, 어떻게 돈을 모으면 좋을까요?

지난번에 우리가 다 같이 쿠키 구워서 팔았을 때 진짜 인기가 아주 좋았잖아요.

이번에도 다 팔 수 있으면 좋겠어요. 좋은 아이디어 좀 제안해 주실래요?

그럼, 이번 주 금요일 오후까지 답장 주시길 바라요.

고맙습니다!

조미수 드림

보내는사람

받는 사람   조미수@mansei.com

참조

제목   RE: 모금 아이디어

첨부

안녕하세요?

<제안> 제 생각에는, _____

_____ (으)면 좋을 것 같아요.

<제안 이유> _____

_____

_____

_____

어때요?

_____ (드림)

모금 fundraising, 아이디어 idea, 올해 this year

2. Welcome to 열린 생각 (Open Thoughts)!

열린 생각 is an online community discussion forum where people can share their candid thoughts, opinions, suggestions, and positions on various topics in the form of posted messages. Post your opinion with supporting ideas.

Follow the guided steps.

New Discussion Topic Posted

일주일에 한 번은 비대면 수업으로 해 주세요!

(1) Fill in the outline chart with your point in a simple sentence.

Argument (your position)	주장: ....
Reasons	1. ....
	2. ....
	3. ....
Suggestion/ Conclusion	제안/결론: ....

(2) Connect each point you wrote down in the outline chart above in three paragraphs using simple sentences.

〈주장〉   저는 ....다고 생각합니다.

〈이유〉   그 이유는 세 가지가 있습니다.

첫째, ...

....

둘째, ...

....

셋째, ...

....

〈제안/결론〉 그러므로, 저는 ....(는 것)을/를 제안합니다.

비대면 virtual, 대면 in-person/face-to-face

Presentational Writing

· The Seoul Metropolitan Office of Education (서울특별시 교육청) in Korea announced a Call-for-Submission for its annual Public Service Announcement (PSA) essay contest. Read the designated topic for the Foreign Students (Beginner Level) division and submit your PSA to win 3,000,000 Won! The top three winners' essays will be made into PSA videos and will air on the Educational Broadcasting Channel.

You may refer to the guided steps in this lesson and Lesson 5. 1.

제 13회 서울시 공익광고 쓰기 대회

외국인 유학생부: 초급

논술 주제: 현재 한국에는 교복을 입어야 되는 중고등학교들도 있고, 사복을 입는 중고등학교들도
있습니다. 그러나 중고등학교 학생들은 모두 교복을 입어야 됩니다.

성명: (한국어)_____ (영문)_____

전화번호:_____

이메일:_____

주소:_____

소속:_____

(주장: 찬성/반대)

(이유: 좋은 점, 나쁜 점)

(제안과 이유)

(결론)

공익광고 public service announcement, 논술 argumentative essay, 제 13회 the 13th (event), −부 division,
중고등학교 middle school and high school, 교복 school uniform, 사복 plain/civilian clothes, 현재 currently,
소속 affiliation, 교육청 office of education

Writing Tips

문장 부호: 쌍점 (:) vs 반쌍점 (;)
Colon vs Semicolon

In Korean writing, ; (반쌍점, semicolon) is not used, unlike in English writing conventions. : (쌍점, colon) is used as in the following examples.

1. when you list things that are included

> `ex` 계절: 봄, 여름, 가을, 겨울

2. when you add brief explanation after a subheading

> `ex` 날짜: 0000년 00월 00일

3. when you write time

> `ex` 오후 10:30 (10시 30분)

문장 접속부사
Sentence Conjunctive Adverbs

Sentence #1 + Conjunctive Adverbs + Sentence #2

Conjunctive adverbs create a flow of text and allow logical development of the text, conveying specific meanings such as contrast (그런데/그러나), consequence (그래서), addition (그리고), and condition (그럼/그러면). Sentence conjunctions in Korean, as adverbs, connect sentences. That is why you can begin your sentence with a conjunction.

Here are some basic differences between these words, although their meanings are the same in dictionaries.

1. 그러나 vs. 그런데 vs. 근데 (But, However)

   그러나 is used in formal writing. 그런데 is used in casual writing and in speaking. 근데 is the colloquial form of 그런데 and is commonly used in speaking and texting.

2. 그러므로 vs. 그래서 (Therefore, Thus)

   Both 그러므로 and 그래서 can be used in writing, but 그러므로 is more formal; therefore, it is not used in casual writing.

3. 그러면 vs. 그럼 (If so)

   These words mean "if so" in English and are used both in writing and speaking in Korean. However, 그럼 is a contracted form of 그러면, so it is not recommended in formal writing in general.

5.4. 설득 Persuasion

Lesson Objectives

- Writing simple text to persuade someone
- Writing to describe and share simple narratives to convince someone

Can-Do

- I can identify basic information presented in simple persuasive texts.
- I can exchange basic persuasive remarks using practiced or memorized words, phrases, and simple sentences.
- I can present my rationale to convince someone on familiar topics in simple/loosely connected sentences.

Useful Vocabulary, Grammar, and Expressions

1. Vocabulary

☐ 설득하다 to persuade   ☐ 믿다 to believe/trust   ☐ 따르다 to follow

☐ 말을 듣다 to listen to (follow someone's opinion)   ☐ 바꾸다 to change

2. Grammar

① N보다 더/덜 more/less than N

② N 중에 가장/제일 the most among N

③ -(으)면 어때요/어떨까요? How about if you ...?

④ 는 게 (더) 좋겠어요. It would be better to

⑤ 는 게 (더) 좋지 않아요? Isn't it better to

⑥ -아/어 주세요. Please do

⑦ -지 마세요. Please don't

3. Expressions

① 다시 (한번만) 생각해 보세요. Please think again (just one more time).

② 이게/그게/저게 더 좋아요. This/that is better.

③ 제 말 좀 들어 보세요. Please try to listen to me.

④ (저를) 한번 믿어 보세요. Please just trust me.

Writing Samples

1. The Ministry of Environment in Korea announced the winners for its annual ***Saving the Earth*** campaign poster competition. Below is the winning poster for the elementary students group.

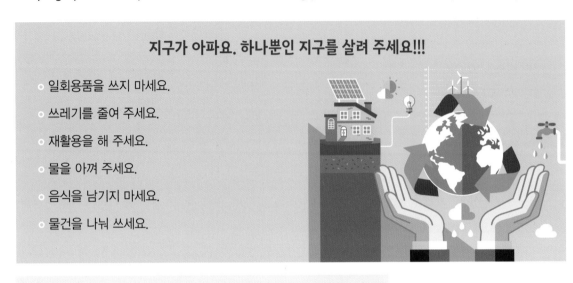

지구 earth, 살리다 to give life, 일회용품 disposables, 쓰레기 trash, 재활용 recycle

2. Woori University is proposing to raise tuition, and a group of students are forming an online petition against this plan. Below includes the students' voices persuading university board members.

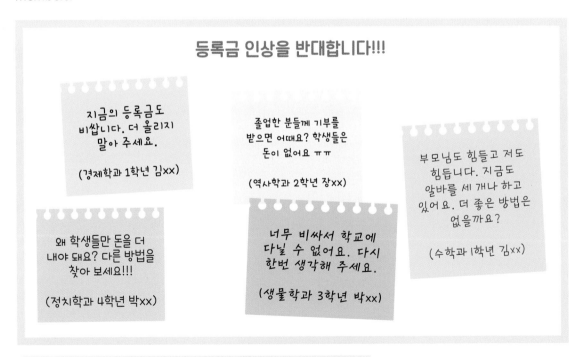

등록금 tuition, 인상 raise, 반대하다 to oppose, 방법 method, 기부 donation

Pre-Writing Exercises

- Your Korean teacher plans to assign project groups based on a trendy game in Korea "Would you rather choose A or B?" (a.k.a. Balance game). You want to be grouped with your best friend and need to choose the same answers for this game. Pick your preference for each category and persuade your friend why your choice is better than the other.

(1) 프라이드 치킨 대(vs) 양념 치킨

  Would you rather order fried chicken OR seasoned chicken?

....

....

....

....

(2) 짜장면 대(vs) 짬뽕

  Would you rather eat black bean sauce noodles OR spicy seafood noodle soup?

....

....

....

....

(3) 탕수육 부먹 (부어 먹기) 대(vs) 찍먹 (찍어 먹기)

  When eating sweet and sour pork, are you pouring sauce OR dipping it?

....

....

....

....

(4) 산 대(vs) 바다

Would you rather spend your vacation at a mountain OR sea?

....
....
....
....

(5) 여름 대(vs) 겨울

Would you rather live always in summer OR always in winter?

....
....
....
....

Interpersonal Writing

1. You need to persuade each friend to do things together. Use various expressions of persuasion (see samples below) and complete the texting messages.

- –(으)면 어때요/어떨까요?
- –는 게 (더) 좋겠어요.
- –는 게 (더) 좋지 않아요?
- 다시 (한번만) 생각해 보세요.

- 이게/그게/저게 더 좋아요.
- 제 말 좀 들어 보세요.
- 한번 (저를) 믿어 보세요.
- 이번에는 제 말대로 해 보세요.

(1) You and Christine took Elementary Korean together this semester. You learned that she plans not to take the sequencing course next semester.

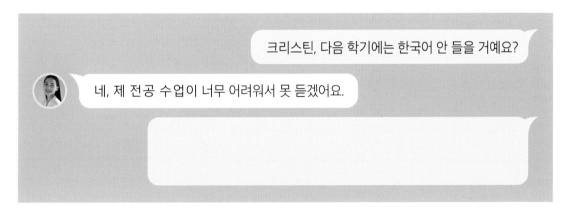

(2) You plan to go to Korea as an exchange student next year. You want to persuade your best friend Eugene to join the program and be roommates in Korea.

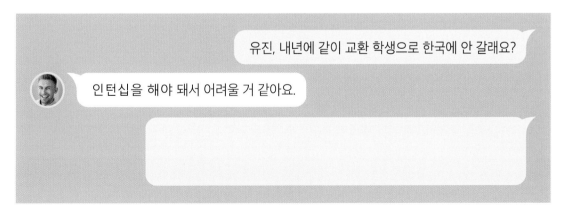

(3) You want to try a backpacking trip to Europe this summer. You are hesitant to go alone, so you decide to persuade your friends from the travel club.

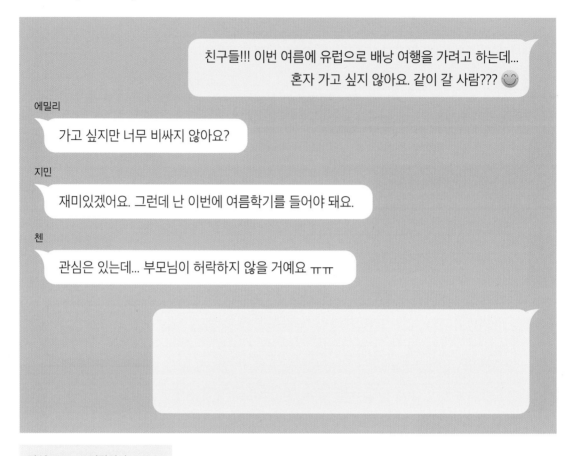

친구들!!! 이번 여름에 유럽으로 배낭 여행을 가려고 하는데... 혼자 가고 싶지 않아요. 같이 갈 사람??? 😊

에밀리
가고 싶지만 너무 비싸지 않아요?

지민
재미있겠어요. 그런데 난 이번에 여름학기를 들어야 돼요.

첸
관심은 있는데... 부모님이 허락하지 않을 거예요 ㅠㅠ

관심 interest, 허락하다 to allow

Presentational Writing

1. You and your date plan to spend time together this weekend but cannot agree with each other for the date plan. Write an email to persuade him/her. Here is the list of each one's preference.

You		Your date
오전에 만나기		오후에 만나기
로맨스 영화 보기		액션 영화 보기
음악 듣기		운동 하기
한국 음식 먹기		미국 음식 먹기

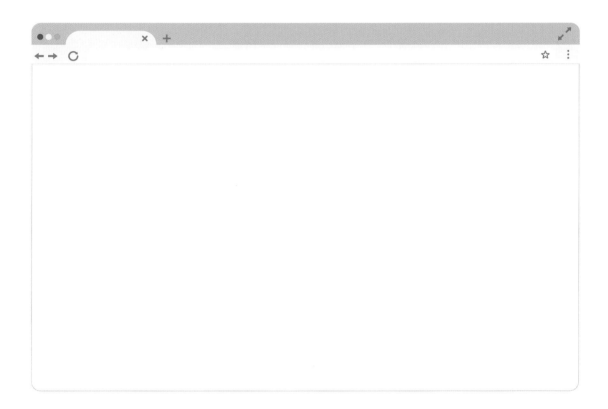

2. You are living with your parents since your home is 30-minutes away from your college. You want to move to an APT near school, but your parents do not allow it and ask you to commute from home. After you mentioned the plan to your mother last night, she left the memo below on your desk today.

학교 근처에 있는 아파트로 이사가고 싶다고?

혼자 살면 음식도 만들어야 하고 청소, 빨래도 다 해야 돼. 그리고 대학원에 갈 돈도 모아야 되는데 아파트는 비싸고 안전하지 않아. 지금은 그냥 집에서 다니는 게 좋겠어.

무엇보다도, 넌 아직 어리니까... 나중에 대학원에 가면 아파트에 사는 게 어때? 아빠 생각도 엄마하고 같아. 주말에 다시 얘기해 보자.

사랑하는 엄마 :-)

돈을 모으다 to save money, 안전하다 to be safe, 무엇보다도 above all, -자 Let's

Your friend advised you to write a hand-written letter which can be a better way to show your sincerity. Write a letter to your parents and persuade them by providing reasonable explanations such as the following.

○ 교통비/시간을 아낀다. 싼 집을 찾을 수 있다. 알바를 한다.
○ 안전하다. 친구와 같이 산다.
○ 요리를 잘 한다. 시장이 가깝다.
○ 대학생이다. 독립하고 싶다.

아버지, 어머니께,

_____

_____

_____

_____

_____

사랑하는 아들/딸 _____ 올림

아끼다 to save, 독립하다 to be independent

간접 표현 #2

Indirect Expressions and Politeness #2

To persuade someone, you will need to use proper and polite expressions.
Instead of direct command, you can use -아/어 주다 to be more polite.

`ex` 가세요. < 가 주세요/주십시오.

Using 겠 can add more politeness for effective persuasion.

`ex` 가 주시면 좋겠어요/좋겠습니다, 가 주시겠어요/주시겠습니까?

Indirect expressions such as -(으)ㄹ 것 같다 can be also used to add politeness.

`ex` 가 주시면 좋을 것 같아요/같습니다.

Sometimes, using questions can sound more polite than using commands or statements.

`ex` 가 주세요. < 가 주실래요? < 가 주시면 어때요/어떨까요/어떻겠습니까?

Lesson Objectives

- Writing simple notices
- Writing to present and exchange simple notices to inform rules or guidelines in daily living (e.g. Do's/ Don'ts in public places and transportations)

Can-Do

- I can identify and interpret simple notices of general/public behaviors (e.g. prohibitions or requirements in public places and transportations) in words, phrases, expressions, simple sentences, and images/signs.
- I can ask for and express a simple and straightforward guide of requirements, requests, or commands on familiar topics in daily living using polite words and expressions in simple sentences.
- I can produce written presentations of simple guidelines/notices/requests in posters, brochures, public notice signs, notes, etc. in simple/loosely connected sentences.

 ## Useful Vocabulary, Grammar, and Expressions

1. Vocabulary

(1)
☐ 안내문/알림 notice	☐ 공지 announcement	☐ 게시판 bulletin board
☐ 안내 guide	☐ 규칙 rule	☐ 금지 prohibition
☐ 금연 no smoking	☐ 담배 피우기/흡연 smoking	☐ 술 마시기/음주 drinking
☐ 이용/사용 use	☐ 반려동물 pet/companion animal	☐ 개 dog

☐ 강아지 puppy	☐ 고양이 cat	☐ 반려견 pet dog
☐ 반려묘 pet cat	☐ 음식물 foods	☐ 반입 bringing
☐ 계단 stairs	☐ 조심/주의 caution	☐ 진동 모드 vibration mode
☐ 음료(수) non-alcohol beverage	☐ 술 liquor	☐ 미끄럼 slip/slippery

(2)
☐ 노크하다 to knock	☐ 조심하다/주의하다 to be careful/cautious	
☐ 미끄럽다 to be slippery	☐ 알리다 to inform	☐ 만지다 to touch
☐ 씻다 to wash	☐ 위험하다 to be dangerous	☐ 안전하다 to be safe
☐ 지키다/따르다 to keep/follow/comply (rules/guidelines)		☐ 어기다 to break/fail to comply
☐ 술(을) 마시다 to drink liquor	☐ 음주하다 to drink liquor	☐ 담배(를) 피우다 to smoke
☐ 흡연하다 to smoke	☐ 사진/비디오 찍다 to take photo/video	☐ 거리두기(하다) distancing
☐ 예방접종(하다) vaccination	☐ 격리(하다) isolation/quarantine	

(3)
☐ 꼭/반드시 for sure	☐ 절대로 never	☐ 가능하면 if possible

2. Grammar

① -(으)세요/-(으)십시오 Please, do

② -지 마세요/마십시오 Please don't

③ -(으)ㅂ시다 Let's

④ -지 맙시다 Let's not

⑤ -(아/어) 주세요 Please, do (for me)

⑥ -(아/어) 주시기 바라요/바랍니다 I hope you can/could

⑦ -(아/어) 주시면 감사하겠습니다 I'd appreciate it if you could

⑧ -(아/어)야 되다 should/must

⑨ -(으)면 안 되다 should not/must not

⑩ -(으)니까 because/since

⑪ N 때문에 due to

3. Expressions

① 부탁드립니다. Thank you in advance. (Lit. I beg you.)

② 이해(해 주시기) 바랍니다. I hope you understand.

③ 이해해 주셔서 감사합니다. Thank you for your understanding.

④ 알려드립니다. Please, note.

⑤ 잘 알겠습니다. Well noted.

Writing Samples

1. Vicky is an international student majoring in communications at Jeju University in Korea. She is conducting her research for her senior essay about public communications, particularly about written notices in various places. Here are some samples of notices she has collected.

2. Kushal is a graduate student at Hankuk University in Korea. This afternoon when he went to the dining hall for lunch, he found the following notice at the dining hall.

학생식당 이용 안내

코로나19 안전을 위해 학생식당 이용을 안내해 드립니다. 협조해 주시기를 부탁드립니다.

- 우리 대학 학생만 들어올 수 있습니다. 학생증을 꼭 보여 주시기 바랍니다.
- 테이블마다 2명씩 앉을 수 있습니다. 앉을 수 있는 자리에만 앉아 주세요.
- 식당에 들어오기 전에, 반드시 코로나19 예방접종 QR 코드를 체크인해야 됩니다.
- 식당 안에 있는 손소독제를 사용해 주세요.
- 식사 전과 후에는 마스크를 꼭 쓰세요.
- 식사 후 일회용 접시, 숟가락, 젓가락을 모두 일회용 쓰레기통에 버리세요.
- 줄 설 때 거리두기를 지켜 주시기 바랍니다.
- 식당 안에 있는 종이컵과 종이 접시는 한 번씩만 사용한 후에 버려 주세요.
- 음식이나 음료수를 리필할 때에는 꼭 새 접시와 새 컵을 사용해야 됩니다.

협조해 주셔서 감사합니다.
한국대학교 학생식당

체크인 check in, 정보 무늬(information pattern)/큐아르코드/QR 코드 QR code,
손소독제 hand sanitizer, 일회용 disposable, 리필 refill, 줄 서다 to be in line

Pre-Writing Exercises

1. Your school is making multilingual notices in some places at your school. You are in charge of the Korean language notices. Prepare each sign with a message (in a sentence) in Korean using the keywords provided for your reference.

❶ .... (물, 셀프)

❷ .... (쓰레기, 버리다)

❸ .... (손, 씻다)

❹ .... (조용하다)

❺ .... (사진/비디오, 찍다)

❻ .... (핸드폰, 진동 모드)

❼ .... (담배, 피우다)

❽ .... (음식, 먹다, 가지고 오다)

❾ .... (거리두기)

❿ .... (마스크, 쓰다)

2. You work as a part-time usher at a local performance theater in Broadway, New York. This theater provides multilingual services and signs for audiences from all over the world. Your responsibilities as an usher include helping the audience find seats, answering general questions, and updating written guidelines in Korean for proper etiquette at the theater. Update the guidelines of theater etiquette for the Korean language part.

Provide the six most important pointers on theater etiquette that the general audience should follow. Write simple, straightforward, and polite guidelines/notices in sentences.

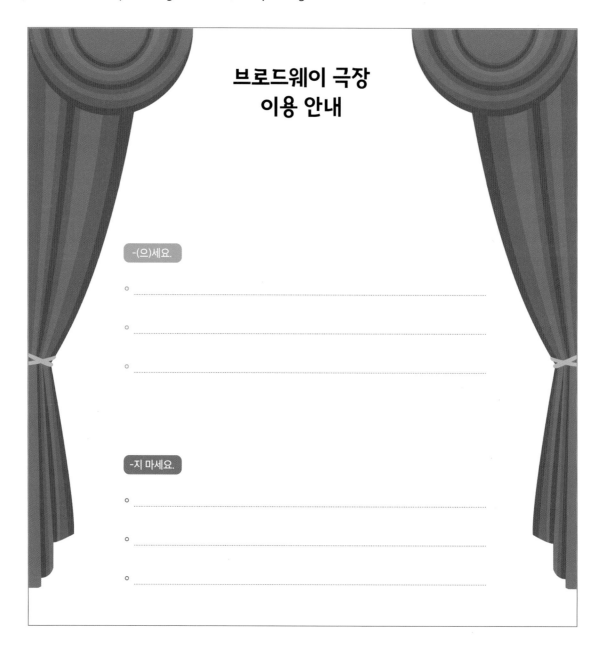

브로드웨이 극장
이용 안내

-(으)세요.

○ ....

○ ....

○ ....

-지 마세요.

○ ....

○ ....

○ ....

Interpersonal Writing

1. You work at a Korean company in Seoul and are excited to take a two-week vacation to visit your family in the U.S. You decided to sublet your apartment to one of the short-term interns in your office while you are on vacation.

   The intern sent you an email with some questions about living in your apartment. Write an email response to the intern providing essential housekeeping information you want him/her/them to keep in mind.

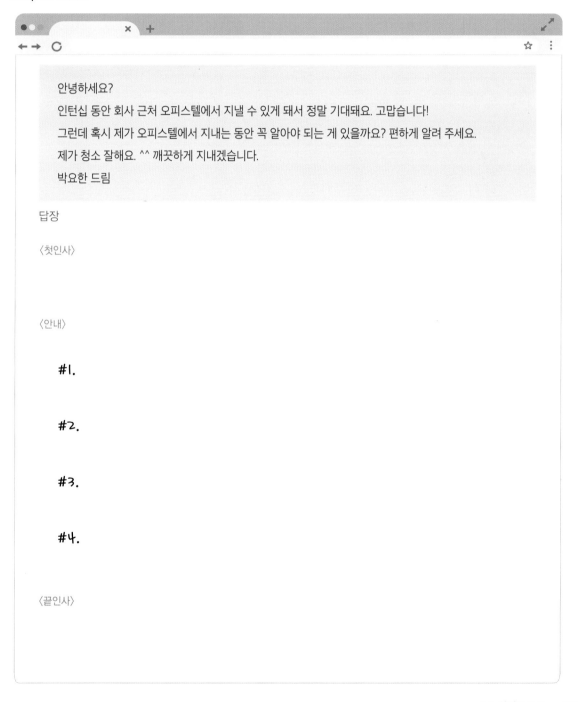

안녕하세요?

인턴십 동안 회사 근처 오피스텔에서 지낼 수 있게 돼서 정말 기대돼요. 고맙습니다!

그런데 혹시 제가 오피스텔에서 지내는 동안 꼭 알아야 되는 게 있을까요? 편하게 알려 주세요.

제가 청소 잘해요. ^^ 깨끗하게 지내겠습니다.

박요한 드림

답장

〈첫인사〉

〈안내〉

    #1.

    #2.

    #3.

    #4.

〈끝인사〉

2. Your new pet sitter is coming this week to take care of your pet(s) for one hour while you are out. Write a note in advance to let the sitter know about your pet(s), helpful tips, and specific service requests for your pet(s).

도우미님, 안녕하세요?

(반려동물 소개)

....

....

....

....

....

(안내: 부탁/요청)

○ ....

○ ....

○ ....

○ ....

○ ....

○ ....

감사합니다. 잘 부탁드려요.

도우미 helper

Presentational Writing

1. The Office of International Students at Hankuk University is updating its guide brochure of living on campus for new members. This academic year, the brochure will include authentic guidance from the current students in the campus community. Add your friendly guide information on the bulletin board to help international students get settled in the community.

국제 학생 커뮤니티 게시판

교내 생활 꿀팁 알림

이번 학기부터 학교 안 우체국에서 돈을 보낼 수 없습니다.
돈을 보내려면 학생 회관 은행을 이용하세요.

점심 시간에 가능하면 사람들이 제일 많이 오는 시간(12:00-12:30)을 피하는 게 좋습니다.

기숙사 안에 술을 가지고 들어가거나 마시면 절대로 안 됩니다!!

통역 서비스 동아리가 있으니까 도움이 필요하면 언제든지 연락해 주세요.
그리고 우리 통역 서비스 동아리에 가입해서 봉사해 주세요.

교내 on campus, 꿀팁 hack/useful tip, 알림 notice, 통역 language interpreting, 피하다 to avoid

2. You are a high school/college student in Korea. Your school's annual club expo will be held soon, and your club is preparing a poster presentation to promote. Your assigned part of the presentation is to make slides to inform all the students who visit your club booth of the club rules and participation guidelines.

동아리:

동아리 규칙/활동 안내

○

○

○

○

○

Writing Tips

어조
Tone of Voice

The tone of voice, such as friendliness, politeness, and formality, in Korean, especially in the writing of general/public notices, can vary depending on the language (the sentence endings, adverbs, etc.) you choose.

- 손 씻어. Wash your hands.
- 손 씻으세요. Please wash your hands. (informal)
- 손 씻으십시오. Please, wash your hands. (formal)
- 손 씻어야 됩니다. You should wash your hands.
- 손을 반드시/꼭 씻어야 됩니다. You absolutely have to/ must wash your hands.
- 손 씻어 주세요. I kindly ask you to wash your hands.
- 손 씻어 주시기 바랍니다. (literally) I want you to wash your hands (for me).
  Thank you for washing your hands in advance.
- 손 씻어 주시기를 부탁드립니다. I ask you to wash your hands, as a favor.
- 손 씻어 주시면 (대단히) 감사하겠습니다. It would be (much) appreciated if you could wash your hands.

As shown in the examples, you may identify some differences in the tone of voice. Although you use imperative sentences to give direct commands or requests, you can provide instructions or guidance more politely, yet still clearly, by using different endings, words, phrases, and expressions.

헷갈리는 띄어쓰기
Confusing Spacing

헷갈리는 맞춤법
Confusing Spelling

헷갈리는 외래어 표기법
Confusing Foreign Word Notation

헷갈리는 띄어쓰기 *Confusing Spacing*

1. Put a space between words.

   `ex` 선생님v지금v어디v계세요?

2. Do not put a space before particles.

   `ex` 유미는v주말에v집에만v있었어요.

   집에서만이라도　　　　　　먹기는커녕

3. Do not put a space before 이다.

   `ex` 저는v학생이에요.　　　이름은v김민지예요.

4. Except for some commonly used single syllable nouns, put a space before demonstrative pronouns.

   `ex` 이/그/저v사람

   이분/그분/저분　　　이때/그때/저때　　　이곳/그곳/저곳

5. Put a space between numbers and counters. This does not apply when using Arabic numerals or indicating orders.

   `ex` 두v시간　　　　　　옷v한v벌

   열v시v삼십v분　　　10시v30분

   1학년　　　　　　　일(v)학년

6. Put a space before negative 안/못 expressions. For ～지 않다/못하다 form, put a space between 지 and 않다/못하다.

   `ex` 안v먹어요　　　　　못v먹어요

   먹지v않아요　　　　먹지v못해요

7. Put a space before dependent nouns.

   a. ‒(으)ㄴ/는/(으)ㄹv것 (thing)

   `ex` 갈v것입니다.　　　갈v겁니다.　　　갈v거예요.

   먹을v게v많아요.　　먹을v건v있어요.　　먹을v걸v주세요.

   올v거v같아요.　　　올v것만v같습니다.

b. ㅡ(으)ㄹ∨수 (ability to)

ex 잘∨수∨있어요.　　　　　　읽을∨수도∨없어요.

c. ㅡ(으)ㄴ∨지 (time since)

ex 만난∨지∨10년∨됐어요.　　밥∨먹은∨지∨한∨시간∨됐어.

d. Verb + ㅡ(으)ㄴ/는/(으)ㄹ∨만큼 (amount)

ex 먹을∨만큼∨만드세요.　　　일한∨만큼∨벌었어요.

e. Verb + ㅡ(으)ㄹ∨뿐 (only)

ex 예쁠∨뿐∨아니라　　　　　　재미있을∨뿐이다

8. It is optional but good practice to put a space between main verbs and helping verbs. There are some cases where two verbs became one word where no space should be used.

ex 도와(∨)줬어요　　　　가져(∨)왔어요　　　　사(∨)놓았어요

올(∨)듯해요　　　　　할(∨)만해요　　　　　먹어(∨)버렸어요

바빠졌어요　　　　　　없어졌어요　　　　　돌아가셨어요

9. Do not put a space for Korean personal proper nouns (e.g., last and first names) unless it is necessary to clarify meaning. Most foreign names have a space between first and last names.

ex 김연아　　　　　　　박세리　　　　이민수∨선생님

황∨보석　　　　　　　황보∨석

스티브∨윌슨　　　　　마이클∨잭슨

10. For non-personal proper nouns, it is optional but good practice to use spaces to clarify meaning.

ex 서울(∨)대학교∨한국어(∨)교육학과

11. It is optional but good practice to use spaces for difficult proper nouns (e.g., specialty or technology terms) to clarify meaning.

ex 만성(∨)골수성(∨)백혈병 (chronic myelocytic leukemia)

헷갈리는 맞춤법 Confusing Spelling

Word/ Expression	Meaning	Correct	Incorrect	Examples
이다	to be	V+예요	에요	이건 피자예요.
		C+이에요	이예요	저는 학생이에요.
아니다	no	아니요	아니오	아니요, 시간이 없어요.
	not	아니에요	아니예요	저는 학생이 아니에요.
-(스)ㅂ니다	deferential ending (statement)	-(스)ㅂ니다	-(으)ㅂ니다	책을 읽습니다.
-(으)십시오	deferential ending (command)	-(으)십시오	-(으)십시요	책을 읽으십시오.
되다	to become	되	돼	되고, 되니까, 되면, 되지만, 됩니다
		되+어=돼	되	돼서, 돼, 돼요, 됐어요, 됐습니다
안	do not	안	않	안 먹어요.
-지 않다	do not	-지 않아요	-지 안아요	먹지 않아요.
-(으)ㄹ게요	will (volition or promise)	-(으)ㄹ게요	-(으)ㄹ께요	제가 갈게요.
-(으)러	in order to	-(으)러	-(으)로	공부하러 도서관에 가요.
-(으)려고	intend to, plan to	-(으)려고	-(으)ㄹ려고	저녁에 불고기를 만들려고 해요.
-던	used to	-던	-든	어릴 때 가던 곳이에요.
-든	either or	-든	-던	가든 말든 마음대로 하세요.
데	place	데	대	좋은 데 알아요?
-(으)ㄴ/는데	but, however	데	대	한국어는 재미있는데 어려워요.
-((느)ㄴ)대	they say that	대	데	한국어는 재미있대요.
-(으)로서	as (role)	-(으)로서	-(으)로써	학생으로서 공부를 열심히 해야지요.
-(으)로써	with, by (means)	-(으)로써	-(으)로서	돈으로써 행복을 살 수 없어요.
며칠	what date; a few days	며칠	몇 일	오늘 며칠이에요?
바쁘다	to be busy	바빠요	바뻐요	요즘 좀 바빠요.
왠지	for no reason	왠지	웬지	오늘은 왠지 좀 피곤해요.

웬일	what matter	웬일	왠일	여기 웬일이세요?
오랜만	long time	오랜만	오랫만	오랜만이에요.
오랫동안	for long	오랫동안	오랜동안	오랫동안 못 만났어요.
바라다	to wish	바라요	바래요	잘 지내길 바라요.
피우다	to smoke; to cheat	피워요	펴요	담배 피워요?
새다	to leak	새요	세요	가방에서 물이 새요.
세다	to count	세요	새요	학생 수를 세요.
새우다	to sit up all night	새워요	새요, 세워요	어제 밤을 새웠어요?
세우다	to set up	세워요	새워요	넘어진 나무를 세워요.
깜박	blink, short moment	깜박		깜박 잊어버렸어요.
깜빡		깜빡		깜빡 잊어버렸어요.
따뜻하다	to be warm	따듯해요		오늘 날씨가 따듯해요.
따듯하다		따뜻해요		오늘 날씨가 따뜻해요.
찌개	stew	찌개	찌게	순두부 찌개 먹을래요.
자장면	black bean noodle	자장면		자장면을 좋아해요.
짜장면		짜장면		짜장면을 좋아해요.
떡볶이	seasoned rice cake	떡볶이	떡복이, 떡뽁이	떡볶이가 맛있어요.
육개장	spicy beef soup	육개장	육계장	육개장은 매워요.
개	dog; item	개	게	개 한 마리가 있어요.
게	crab	게	개	게는 바다에 살아요.
채	as it is	채	체	못 본 채 그냥 갔어요.
체	pretending	체	채	보고도 못 본 체 그냥 갔어요.
잊어버리다	to forget	잊어버려요	잃어버리다	숙제하는 걸 잊어버렸어요.
잃어버리다	to lose	잃어버려요	잊어버리다	숙제한 걸 잃어버렸어요.
부치다	to mail	부쳐요	붙여요	편지를 부쳤어요.
붙이다	to attach	붙여요	부쳐요	메모를 게시판에 붙였어요.

헷갈리는 외래어 표기법 Confusing Foreign Word Notation

Foreign Words	Correct	Incorrect
accessory	액세서리	악세사리
ad lib	애드리브	애드립
air conditioner	에어컨	에어콘
badge	배지	뺏지
barbecue	바비큐	바베큐, 비비큐
battery	배터리	밧데리, 빳데리
biscuit	비스킷	비스켓
body	보디	바디
Boston	보스턴	보스톤
buffet	뷔페	부페
business	비즈니스	비지니스
café	카페	까페
cake	케이크	케잌, 케익
cardigan	카디건	가디건
catalog	카탈로그	카다로그, 카탈록
center	센터	쎈터
chance	찬스	챤스, 챈스
chocolate	초콜릿	초컬릿, 초콜렛, 쵸코렛
coffee	커피	코피, 카피
collection	컬렉션	콜렉션
concert	콘서트	컨서트
condition	컨디션	콘디숀, 콘디션
contents	콘텐츠	컨텐츠
copy	카피	코피, 커피
curtain	커튼	커텐
encore	앙코르	앙콜, 앵콜
family	패밀리	패미리, 훼미리

fan	팬	펜
fighting	파이팅	화이팅
file	파일	화일
film	필름	필림
flash	플래시	후레시, 후레쉬
fresh	프레시	프레쉬, 후레쉬, 후레시
frypan	프라이팬	후라이판, 후라이팬
gas range	가스레인지	가스렌지
gown	가운	까운
highlight	하이라이트	하일라이트
Halloween	핼러윈	핼로윈, 할러윈, 할로윈
Hollywood	할리우드	할리웃, 헐리웃, 헐리우드
internship	인턴십	인턴쉽
juice	주스	쥬스
leadership	리더십	리더쉽
leisure	레저	레져
Los Angeles	로스앤젤레스	로스엔젤레스
makeup	메이크업	메이컵
mania	마니아	매니아
market	마켓	마켇, 마켙, 마케트
massage	마사지	맛사지, 마싸지, 맛싸지
mattress	매트리스	맷트리스, 메트리스
Mozart	모차르트	모짜르트
network	네트워크	네트웍, 네트웤
New York	뉴욕	뉴요크, 뉴욬
nonsense	난센스	넌센스
nosebleed	코피	커피, 카피
pamphlet	팸플릿	팜플렛
pan	팬	펜
panda	판다	팬더, 팬다
Paris	파리	빠리, 패리스
pen	펜	팬

pizza	피자	피짜, 핏자, 핏짜
placard	플래카드	플랭카드
plaza	플라자	프라자
racket	라켓	라켙, 라켙, 라케트
radar	레이더	레이다
radio	라디오	레디오, 래디오
robot	로봇	로보트
royal	로열	로얄
sash	새시	샤시, 샷시
sausage	소시지	소세지
service	서비스	써비스
set	세트	셋트, 셑
shop	숍	숖, 샵
sofa	소파	쇼파
soup	수프	스프, 슾
special	스페셜	스페샬
staff	스태프	스탭, 스탶
sunglass	선글라스	썬그라스, 썬글라스, 썬글래스
super	슈퍼	수퍼
supermarket	슈퍼마켓	수퍼마켓, 슈퍼마케트
symbol	심벌	심볼
talent	탤런트	탈렌트
tape	테이프	테프, 테입, 테잎
television	텔레비전	텔레비젼, 테레비전, 테레비
terminal	터미널	터미날
ton kasu	돈가스	돈까스, 돈가쓰
trot	트로트	트롯
Valentine Day	밸런타인 데이	발렌타인 데이
Washington	워싱턴	워싱톤, 와싱턴, 와싱톤
window	윈도	윈도우
workshop	워크숍	워크샵, 웍샵, 웍숍